Earthquake Insurance

Earthquake Insurance

A Longitudinal Study of California Homeowners

Risa Palm

Westview Press
BOULDER • SAN FRANCISCO • OXFORD

This Westview softcover edition is printed on acid-free paper and bound in library-quality, coated covers that carry the highest rating of the National Association of State Textbook Administrators, in consultation with the Association of American Publishers and the Book Manufacturers' Institute.

Published in 1995 in the United States of America by Westview Press, Inc., 5500 Central Avenue, Boulder, Colorado 80301-2877, and in the United Kingdom by Westview Press, 36 Lonsdale Road, Summertown, Oxford OX2 7EW

A CIP catalog record is available for this book from the Library of Congress.
ISBN 0-8133-8898-8

Printed and bound in the United States of America

The paper used in this publication meets the requirements of the American National Standard for Permanence of Paper for Printed Library Materials Z39.48-1984.

10 9 8 7 6 5 4 3 2 1

For John Richard Greenland

Contents

Tables and Figures

Tables

Figures

Acknowledgments

This monograph is based upon work supported by the National Science Foundation under grant no. BCS-92006891. The 1989 survey and the 1990 survey, both referred to in the text, were supported by the National Science Foundation under grant nos. BCS-8802896, BCS-8943381, and BCS-9003573. Any opinions, findings, and conclusions or recommendations expressed in this material are those of the author and do not necessarily reflect the views of the National Science Foundation.

The research assistants who worked on the 1993 survey were John Carroll, Robb Kirkman, and Tom Kochevar. The graduate assistants worked on every aspect of the project execution, the design of the survey instrument, planning of the advisory committee meeting, execution of the mail survey, compilation of findings, development of statistical tests, and production of cartographic and illustrative material. Carroll was the senior research assistant on the project, and I am particularly grateful to John for his leadership and his consistently cheerful can-do attitude throughout this project.

Debbie Rauch worked tirelessly on every aspect of the project research, particularly on the problems of manuscript production. I appreciate her very valuable contributions. Patricia Peterson copyedited the manuscript.

Michael Hodgson was an intellectual partner in the 1989 and 1990 portions of this research and was an inspiration to me concerning the applicability of Geographic Information Systems (GIS) to natural hazards research.

I wish to thank the advisory committee that worked on the 1993 survey design and its mid-term evaluation. Their advice and assistance were invaluable. Members of this committee were: Jane Bullock of the Federal Emergency Management Agency; Frank Reilly of the Federal Emergency Management Agency-Federal Insurance Administration; Dick Roth of the California Insurance Department; Gene LeComte of the National Committee on Property Insurance; Tom

Tobin of the California Seismic Safety Commission; Howard Kunreuther of the Wharton School, University of Pennsylvania; Joanne Nigg of the Disaster Research Center, University of Delaware; Paul Slovic of Decision Research in Eugene, Oregon; Brian Stoner of the California Seismic Safety Commission; Sal Bianco of Fremont Pacific Insurance Group; and Bill Gage, aid to Cecil Green, the California State Senate.

There were many who provided intellectual guidance and help throughout the course of this project. Just a few of these people include David Greenland, Gilbert White, and Joe Stone.

Most of all, I wish to thank Bill Anderson of the National Science Foundation for his continuing intellectual guidance, support, and very helpful advice. Without his guidance, this work would surely not have been completed.

Risa Palm

1

Natural Hazards

Introduction

On January 17, 1994, southern California was reminded of the power of an earthquake to disrupt life and destroy property. In the 1994 San Fernando earthquake, more than sixty people died, 5000 were injured and 25,000 were left homeless (Figure 1.1). It was the most destructive earthquake within the United States since the 1906 San Francisco earthquake, with damage estimates over $20 billion.

More serious threats are the "great earthquakes" predicted for the San Andreas fault in southern California (magnitude 8.3) and for the Newport-Inglewood fault, which bisects downtown Los Angeles (magnitude 7.5). Depending on the time of day, such earthquakes could cause many thousands of deaths and direct economic losses in excess of $70 billion.

Can people protect themselves from these very destructive events? The answer is "yes." At the county or city level, people can adapt land use and construction standards to known geological conditions and earthquake probabilities. For example, certain classes of rock or soil are more subject to shaking or failure, increasing the potential for damage to roads or buildings. By combining maps of more vulnerable areas with information about the likelihood of earthquakes in various regions, local jurisdictions can plan land use in response to known hazards.

Individuals can protect themselves against some of the worst effects of an earthquake that occur in the first 72-hour emergency period. California residents and visitors can learn about protective measures from a large number of sources. For example, telephone books describe emergency procedures to follow during and immediately after an earthquake. California state law requires real estate agents to provide purchasers of pre-1960 homes with copies of "The

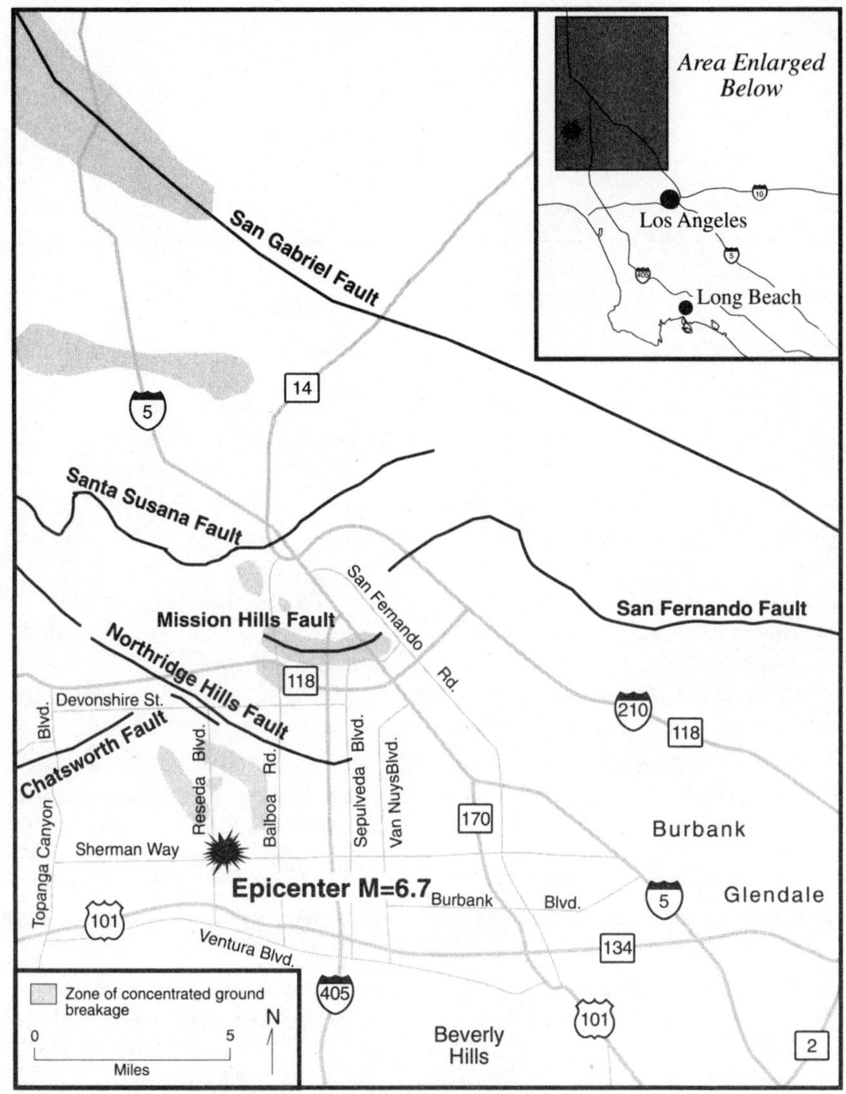

FIGURE 1.1 Map of 1994 San Fernando earthquake

Homeowner's Guide to Earthquake Safety," a booklet containing information on geologic and seismic hazards and recommendations for mitigating the hazards. In addition, many agencies distribute brochures, maps, scientific reports and other materials on the earthquake hazard and mitigation measures.

Yet, despite an immense effort invested in understanding seismic risk and providing information about appropriate actions, many

Americans remain unresponsive to the earthquake hazard until their own home is damaged, their own job is lost, or members of their own family are injured or killed. Why do individuals and communities ignore this geophysical risk? This question is the subject of this book.

The studies presented here focus on one specific lens through which one can view the response of individuals and households to earthquake hazard: the decision by homeowners to purchase earthquake insurance.

Theory of Hazard Response

What factors predict that homeowners will purchase earthquake insurance? This question is a more specific form of the general question of how individuals respond to uncertainties in their environment. This issue--the relationship of individuals to hazards in the environment--is the subject of a great deal of empirical research.

Empirical Findings

Survey research has explored the relationship between environmental response and a long series of empirical factors. Among the factors linked with the response of Americans to environmental uncertainties are equity position in the house, income level, age, gender, objective geophysical risk, and prior experience with the hazard. We will briefly review a sample of the findings suggesting these associations.

Equity. Anderson and Weinrobe (1981) show that people with the most to lose--those with relatively high net equity in their homes--purchase insurance. Households with high net equity positions tend to protect their investment (Anderson and Weinrobe, 1981; Willinger, 1989).

Income. Income may also affect insurance adoption. Although this variable may not have a simple independent relationship with insurance adoption (Kunreuther et al. 1978), income should modify the direct relationship between net equity and insurance purchase. In California, households often have a high net equity position (for example, only a small mortgage on a property that was once purchased for $35,000, but is now worth $200,000) and yet do not have sufficient monthly income to afford insurance premiums. House-rich, income-poor households sometimes result from the astounding rate of inflation in house prices in California's urban areas over the past 15 years. A number of respondents state that "it is not the house but the land which is worth so much money." In such cases, the direct relationship between net equity and insurance purchase may be modified by income level.

Age. Older homeowners may be more likely to purchase insurance than younger households. This argument is based on two principles concerning risk averse behavior (Arrow, 1970). First, retired heads of households are more likely to have high net equity with low monthly incomes and little prospect for the future accumulation of household wealth. In this case, the purchase of earthquake insurance is necessary to protect the value of the home, the major repository of household wealth. Second, the elderly are generally more likely to adopt adjustments to hazards. For example, Myra Schiff (1977) observes a "high correlation between age and the tendency to adopt adjustments," which "suggests that the adoption of adjustments becomes habitual and is cumulative." Individuals learn about their environments as they live in an area over time, and once they make an adjustment--such as the purchase of insurance--it becomes part of their repertoire. Over time, people learn from environmental cues and make appropriate adjustments.

Gender. Gender may also affect both risk perception and response to environmental hazards, although Cutter et al. (1992:141) conclude that based on empirical studies, "it is virtually impossible to determine what kind of gender perception differences might exist."

Objective Geophysical Risk. Simple proximity to areas at risk may increase the probability of response, including the adoption of insurance. This tendency of people most at risk to want to purchase insurance is known by the insurance industry as "adverse selection." Proximity to the risk is said to bring about higher levels of concern (Greene, Perry, and Lindell, 1981), although this empirical finding does not hold in every case (Geipel, 1982).

Prior Experience. Prior experience with a natural hazard may be linked with adoption of mitigation measures such as insurance purchase. First, personal experience may affect the estimated likelihood of future victimization since accessibility from memory will influence probability judgments (Kahneman and Tversky, 1979; Perloff, 1983). Experience with the earthquake may also be linked with insurance purchase for a second reason: experience reduces uncertainty about the event (Fazio and Zanna, 1978) and demonstrates that individuals are not invulnerable (Janoff-Budman, 1985; Perloff, 1983; Weinstein, 1987). After experiencing an earthquake, a person may realize the potential for damage and the way in which insurance can mitigate some of the economic impacts.

Empirical studies have found conflicting patterns of perceived risk as a function of experience. Windham et al. (1978) and also Baker

(1979) found that newcomers rather than longer-term residents were more likely to evacuate in a hurricane. Meltsner (1978) also found that length of residence in a place reduced perceived risk from earthquakes. In contrast, Cross (1990), in a longitudinal study of residents of the Florida Keys, found that longer-term residents tended to express more rather than less concern about hurricanes. Empirical evidence linking length of residence in a place with concern about environmental hazards is clearly mixed.

Decision Theory

Another line of research, more theoretically based, goes beyond individual characteristics or experience to describe the process of decision-making with respect to environmental risk. The focus is understanding the way in which information is processed and decisions about an uncertain world are undertaken.

The simplest theoretical framework of predicting the purchase of earthquake insurance is an analysis of the ratio of benefits to costs: it would be possible to assess the probable losses to a given property in a given year, and calculate the relative costs of purchasing insurance vs. paying for repairs. This type of cost-benefit analysis is a classical way of analyzing human response to an uncertain environment. For this type of theory to predict not only the "ideal" practice but also the observed practice, the decision-maker must have goals to maximize utility or net benefits in an uncertain world and must possess all relevant information about costs and benefits. Since these assumptions about omniscience cannot be met in an uncertain world, this conceptualization is modified into one of expected utility rather than absolute utility in decision making, particularly with respect to insurance purchase (Mosteller and Nogee, 1941; Friedman and Savage, 1948; Edwards, 1955).

However, even with this modification, empirical studies show that besides a lack of total information, decision-makers have other impediments to simple cost-benefit analysis. The most important impediment is that decision-makers have multiple objectives in the decision process. As a result, the notion of "satisficing" is introduced to describe less-than-perfect strategies along with the specification of individual "errors" in environmental interpretation (Slovic et al. 1977; Kunreuther et al. 1978).

Among the persistent "errors" identified in empirical studies of response to environmental uncertainties are: (1) the gambler's fallacy, (2) editing, and (3) anchoring and adjustment. The gambler's fallacy is the belief that if a low-probability event has occurred recently, it is unlikely to occur again soon and therefore can be treated as an event with a probability of zero (Slovic, Kunreuther and White, 1974). Editing occurs when individuals reduce low probability events to zero (Slovic et al. 1977; Kahneman and Tversky, 1979). Anchoring and adjustment is the tendency to estimate the loss at a particular level and then to adjust estimates around this first approximation--an approximation that may be highly inaccurate and bias later estimates (Tversky and Kahneman, 1974; Einhorn and Hogarth, 1985).

In short, the notion that individuals calculate the costs and benefits of various alternatives and decide on some set of "rational" adaptations to the environment does not fit the empirical reality of complexity in decision-making. Not only do individuals not have complete knowledge of alternatives, but many other factors, including patterns of consistent "errors" in risk calculation, affect decision-making.

Kunreuther et al. (1993:17) discuss decision theory as specifically related to insurance purchase. They argue that individuals tend to make complex trade-offs between such issues as the probability of the event or its likely outcomes, depending on the context of the problem and the mode with which information is communicated: "people often weight these dimensions differently than would be suggested by normative models of choice such as expected utility theory or benefit cost analysis." Two reasons why people tend to show little interest in adopting insurance against natural hazards are (1) a belief that the very low probability event actually has a probability of zero--that it "cannot happen to me"; and (2) a "myopic" time horizon--planning behavior that takes only a few months or years into account rather than the actual estimated time that an individual will be exposed to the hazard. Indeed, the decision to purchase earthquake insurance is a specific example of what Hogarth and Kunreuther label "decision-making under ignorance," where both costs and benefits are unknown to the decision-maker. In such conditions, these authors argue, "people determine choices by using arguments that do not quantify the risk and may reflect concerns that are not part of standard models of choice under uncertainty" (Hogarth and Kunreuther, 1993:2). Instead, people use arguments to justify their decisions that may seem far-fetched or distant from "rational" models of choice.

Cultural Contexts

Individual decision-making takes place in cultural contexts that constrain and enable the range of available choices. The cultural context may, even in the absence of other factors, increase or reduce awareness of risk, and condition the range of acceptable responses.

Wildavsky and Dake (1990) note that personality structures are neither risk-averse nor risk-taking in all situations and therefore that tests of such factors cannot predict hazard response. Instead, "cultural biases provide predictions of risk perceptions and risk-taking preferences that are more powerful than measures of knowledge and personality" (Wildavsky and Dake, 1990:171-172).

A specific example of the impacts of cultural context on hazard response is the research related to "optimism." A number of studies suggest that Americans estimate that they live longer than other people, they are younger for their age than others, and that they are less likely to die from cardiovascular diseases or accidents (Myers, 1992). Garrison Keilor illustrates this belief when he says sardonically that all children of Lake Wobegon are "above average." Researchers find an absence of this optimistic bias in self-perception among Japanese college students (Markus and Kitayama, 1991). This cultural difference in the degree of optimism about personal well-being could also affect perceived vulnerability and the propensity to take risk-mitigating actions.

Many other examples illustrate the ways in which specific aspects of culture affect perceived vulnerability to environmental hazards or the likelihood of the adoption of preparedness. For example, the Church of the Latter Day Saints (Mormon) recommends the storage of food and water, a practice that prepares church members for disasters including earthquakes. Buddhism provides another cultural perspective by suggesting that death or destruction from a natural hazard may be pre-ordained by an individual's previous life. Nonetheless, this perspective demands that the individual take all possible measures to minimize injury or death (Kyoko Tokano, personal communication, 1994). Ancient Chinese cosmology suggested that natural disasters were caused by bad government or a loss of virtue by the state, providing impetus for the government to minimize disaster impacts in order to maintain the appearance of harmony between the ruling order and nature (Suttmeier, 1994).

At the local level, within the United States, boosterism may reflect local culture and affect response to hazards information. Promotion of the local community by real estate owners or developers may overwhelm the influence of scientific information about earthquake hazards: for example, a debate took place between representatives of the US Geological Survey and residents of Ventura County, California over whether a surface fault trace ran through a populated portion of the county. Scientists argued that it did, whereas developers, worrying about property values, denied the validity of the information (Robert Alexander, personal communication, 1978).

Other examples are legion and they reflect the very complex way in which aspects of culture can affect perceived risk and probable response.

Locale and Environment

Recent work in human geography emphasizes the importance of "locale" or local area in interpreting human response to the environment and society. Although the study of "locale" has a long tradition within geography, dating at least from the French *Annales* school of thought, this concept has been re-emphasized with the translation of "post-modern" thought into human geography.

An important insight that a post-modern perspective lends to the study of natural hazards is its tendency to emphasize process within the local area. As Marden (1992:43) states: "the notion that social practice can only be conceived and understood within the confines of local contexts is a powerful motif in postmodernist thought." Locality or local place must be studied for its influence on meaning, whether this meaning is the interpretation of language, the nature of the landscape, or the interpretation of environment. This "interpretive geography" aims at an understanding of intersubjective meanings within social life and criticizes the notion that the major goal of research is to seek general theory or large-scale regularities. Instead, individuals within small groups and within particular places create a separate and individualized pattern of communication. Not only is knowledge interpreted and re-invented in the local area, but, in addition, the local area and its identity become the equivalent of individual identity. Because there are so many sources of knowledge, image, and influence, the local area has an enhanced role in translating and mediating these influences as sources of individual identity (Harvey, 1989:302):

> *Place-identity*, in this collage of superimposed spatial images that implode in upon us, becomes an important issue, because everyone occupies a space of individuation (a body, a room, a home, a shaping community, a nation), and how we individuate ourselves shapes identity. Furthermore, if no one "knows their place" in this shifting collage world, then how can a secure social order be fashioned or sustained.

This emphasis on local context is not new to geography: scholars such as Lukermann (1961) emphasized the importance of local circumstance and "contingency" in modifying the then-popular trend to develop "grand theory." Similarly, post-modern thought suggests that geographic interpretation demands an awareness of the local context.

General overarching theory can not predict the "discourse" or the knowledge system at a particular site; instead, each local context is a place where general systems are interpreted and reinterpreted to create new meaning (Harvey, 1989:45):

> There is an intimate relation between the systems of knowledge ("discourses") which codify techniques and practices for the exercise of social control and domination within particular localized contexts. The prison, the asylum, the hospital, the university, the school, the psychiatrist's office, are all examples of sites where a dispersed and piecemeal organization of power is built up independently of any systematic strategy of class domination. What happens at each site cannot be understood by appeal to some overarching general theory.

Practice at the local level can not be predicted from the overall structure or from random and individual deviations. Instead, a collage of rapidly changing and chaotic influences are integrated in local understandings and processes.

What are the implications of an emphasis on "locale" for the study of natural hazards? At the very least, it suggests that caution must be exercised in applying any single theoretical perspective, in attempting to understand response of people to environmental hazard unless that perspective includes aspects of locale. It is insufficient to look for statistical associations of individual or variable combinations (income, education, past experience) with perceived vulnerability and hazard response. Although such tests must be performed, they are inevitably incomplete since they omit unique aspects of locale. Even a model or theory that integrates conditions of the political economy and cultural interpretations of hazard with such variable complexes is insufficient: although such models are useful in sketching the overall picture, one must not forget that response in a given place is contingent upon and a function of a combination of the specific characteristics of the locale interacting with more general structural processes. This insight of post-modern theory adds to and enriches our perspective on hazards geography.

Integrative Model

An integrative model, including generalizations linking political economy, cultural context, locale and individual variability, can describe in a general way the response to environmental hazard. This model notes that all human societies confront a physical environment that is constantly changing as a result of geophysical processes and human activity. Given the fact that variability in the physical environment is part of the context within which human life is played out, the question becomes: At what point does environmental variability become transformed from a neutral process to one perceived as "hazardous"? And when do hazardous environments become the target for public policy?

The integrative model is divided into two stages. In the first stage, geophysical events--environmental variability and change--become transformed into "hazards." In the second stage, the environmental hazard is translated into individual action.

Stage I: Environmental Variability Becomes Environmental Hazard

At least five conditions are necessary for the transformation of an otherwise neutral change in the physical environment into a threat requiring action by of individuals or governmental bodies. First, appropriate authorities must become aware of the occurrence of a large number of deaths, injuries, or property losses attributed to a particular environmental source. It is not enough that these losses occur; they must also be seen as "caused" by an environmental agent. This process must be recognized by an authority that has the power to act on these losses. In addition, the response is affected not only by the particular incident, but also by the extent to which it seems to portend costs or future losses--the signal potential of the event.

Second, the political economic structure (governmental unit, for example) must have sufficient resources to deal with the problem. Resources in this sense include not only the economic means to provide relief or plan mitigation schemes but also the political-social organization to muster human resources to address the issue. In the contemporary world, relatively more affluent and politically stable societies will perceive and respond to environmental hazards more quickly and effectively than less affluent societies.

Third, the culture must accept that individuals or collectivities have the ability and the responsibility to control the physical environment. If the culture is pervaded by a belief that environmental disaster is inevitable, natural and not subject to human control, people will be less likely to take action to mitigate against environmental disaster. Societies that hold the belief that they are responsible for controlling or managing the physical environment are far more proactive than those that rely on the will of a supreme being, on chance, or on luck to explain why some people prosper and others suffer losses.

A related factor is the set of beliefs within a culture about appropriate society-environment interactions. The ends of this continuum are, on the one hand, the belief in humans as "conquerors" or the environment in service of human activity, and, on the other, the belief in human activity as a natural part of the environment, in symbiosis. Although no modern society falls at one or the other extreme of this continuum, societies vary greatly in the extent to which the environment is seen as controllable. It should be noted that those societies that depend on large-scale technological projects to "manage" risk may, in the process, increase the risk from very large-scale disasters (dam failures, for example).

A fourth factor is the set of ethical assumptions within the political-economic system about the responsibility for protecting others from harm. In the United States, the legal assumption is that no one may impose life-threatening risks on others without their consent. Actions fall short of this ethical ideal, however, and frequently actions taken to limit the impacts of hazards on individuals and society may simply redistribute their risk, imposing even greater hazards on others. The extent to which this ethical principle guides actual behavior affects the degree to which environmental hazards are reduced or exacerbated.

Fifth, authorities must accept the idea that they have an ethical responsibility to take action to prevent economic losses, injuries or deaths. There are varying opinions about the role that government should play in mediating environmental-society relationships. In the United States, citizens usually prefer the government to intervene only where individual action is very costly or impossible, or where other organizations cannot protect individuals from risk. In other societies, citizens may have a greater desire for a centralized response to environmental risk.

This variability in perceived responsibility may also be observed at the level of risk managers. Individuals in government or private enterprise charged with responsibility for hazard mitigation vary in the extent to which they understand and respond to their duties. Some managers are lifelong residents of an area and take a personal interest in environmentally sensitive policies; others may not share these personal goals and may ignore or minimize environmental issues.

Stage 2: Environmental Hazard Is Translated into Individual Action

Once the environmental hazard has been "created," that is, that environmental variability and change are perceived as a hazard threatening the well-being of the community, seven additional conditions are necessary before individuals or households will translate perception into action.

First, individuals must become aware of the hazard. The ways in which risks are communicated within a society can affect their salience, and therefore the extent to which people respond to them. Hazards are more likely to be important if they are communicated in a memorable way (individuals can get a vivid picture in their minds of the impacts of the hazard), and if disaster is understood as a high probability event.

Second, individuals must not only perceive the hazard, but also see it as a relatively important part of their daily lives. Since individuals face many problems in contemporary society, it is not enough for a hazard simply to be added to the long list of potential worries. Instead, it must become salient to the household, at least long enough for the household to take some kind of action.

Third, individuals must believe that they can take actions that will actually affect their own safety. If they believe that the event is inevitable, that all residents of their community will be affected, and that the individual can do nothing, they are also likely to do nothing to protect themselves or their families.

Fourth, individuals must perceive themselves as personally vulnerable to property losses or personal injury for them to respond. Within the Euro-American culture, individual differences in perceived vulnerability to hazards greatly affect the probability that individuals or groups will adopt mitigation measures. Here, perceived vulnerability is at least partly related to past experience with the hazard as well as to other variations in related dimensions of personality. Some evidence indicates that this relationship may not hold across cultures--that individual perceived vulnerability may have less impact than societal consensus in cultures that place greater stress on societal connections as opposed to individual achievement.

Fifth, individuals or households must have the resources to respond. Telling individuals to bolt their foundations to the walls or store food is not enough. Households must also have sufficient resources to invest in improved home safety or hazard preparedness.

Sixth, household dynamics and decision-making affect the ways in which household units respond. An individual who is relatively powerless in the household (a child, an elderly parent, a spouse) may perceive the risk and be motivated to act. However, this individual must also be in a position to affect household decision-making for this motivation to be converted into action.

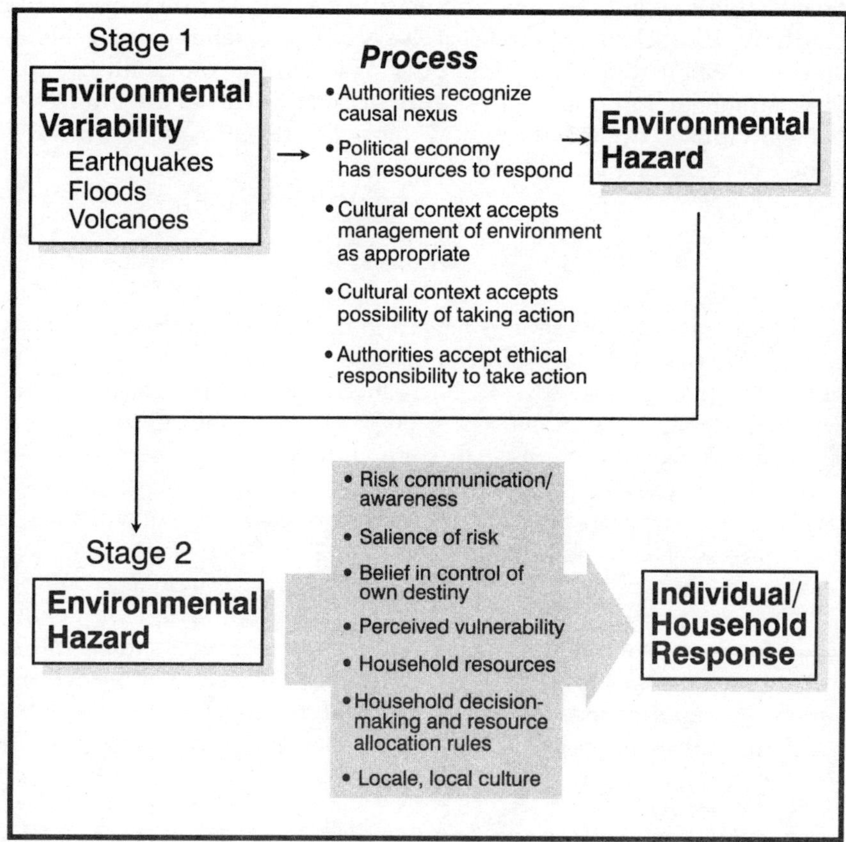

FIGURE 1.2 Integrative model of hazards response

Finally, some variability in individual or collective response is introduced by the nature of the "locale" or the local area within which the hazard exists. Perception of "what people do here," which is a factor quite apart from the overall cultural context, affects perceived vulnerability and beliefs about appropriate response. Local tradition and beliefs about a place can have important effects in the transmission of environmental beliefs and the nature of response.

This inventory of factors affecting the creation of "hazard" and the translation of hazard into response is not complete. It demonstrates, however, the difficulties in predicting the point at which society pays attention and devotes resources to dealing with environmental hazards. The schematic model of this set of constraining and enabling factors demonstrates the complexity of individual/societal/environmental interaction (Figure 1.2). Any decision involves the interaction of individuals, organizations and the political economy, entities that often have different goals and objectives.

Conclusion

Earthquakes pose a serious hazard to millions of Americans, putting at risk billions of dollars of property and thousands of lives. The risk to individual households can be reduced by a variety of mitigation measures, ranging from household preparedness to the adoption of special earthquake insurance. Although earthquake risk and mitigation measures are well publicized, a relatively low percentage of homeowners are prepared for disaster. In this monograph, we will explore the nature of the earthquake hazard and the availability of insurance, and report on a longitudinal study of homeowners in four California counties to chart their growing concern with earthquakes, their increasing tendency to adopt mitigation measures, and yet their continuing overall level of under-preparedness. Finally, we will explore the implications of these empirical findings for public policy and our understanding of human response to environmental hazards.

2

Earthquake Hazards

Earthquakes and faulting affect vast portions of the world, placing hundreds of millions of people at risk. More than 3000 earthquakes occur each year, although most do not involve significant damage or loss of life (Alexander, 1992). Some of the most devastating earthquakes in the historical record took place in China, where an earthquake in 1556 in Shensi claimed 830,000 lives, and another in 1976 claimed 650,000 lives.

In the 20th century, the highest magnitude earthquakes have occurred along the western edges of the North and South American plates, as well as on the western edge of the Pacific Plate and in China (Bryant, 1991). In the United States, these include the San Francisco earthquake of 1906 and the very damaging Fairbanks, Alaska earthquake of 1964 (Table 2.1). Other particularly destructive earthquakes, in terms of loss of life and property, have occurred in Morocco,

TABLE 2.1 High Richter-Magnitude Earthquakes in the 20th Century

Year	Location	Magnitude
1906	Colombia	8.6
1906	Chile	8.4
1906	San Francisco	8.2
1911	Tienshan, China	8.4
1920	Kansu, China	8.5
1923	Tokyo	8.2
1933	Japanese trench	8.5
1950	India	8.6
1960	Chile	8.3
1964	Alaska	8.6
1977	Indonesia	8.9

Chile, Peru, Nicaragua, Guatemala, Indonesia, the Philippines, Turkey, Iran, Algeria and Italy. In each event, many thousands of deaths took place, along with many injuries, serious disruption of communities, and massive property loss.

Fires associated with major earthquakes have claimed large numbers of lives. In the 1906 San Francisco earthquake, about 80 percent of the damage was caused by fire rather than ground shaking; similarly in the 1923 Tokyo earthquake, 160,000 people died, primarily in the intense fires caused by the use of charcoal braziers in wooden houses.

In the United States, earthquakes accompanied with losses of life have occurred in South Carolina, Alaska, Montana, Washington, and California (Figure 2.1). Other states at risk from major damaging earthquakes are Oregon, Utah, the central portion of the Mississippi Valley region around New Madrid, Missouri, and the New England region centering on Boston.

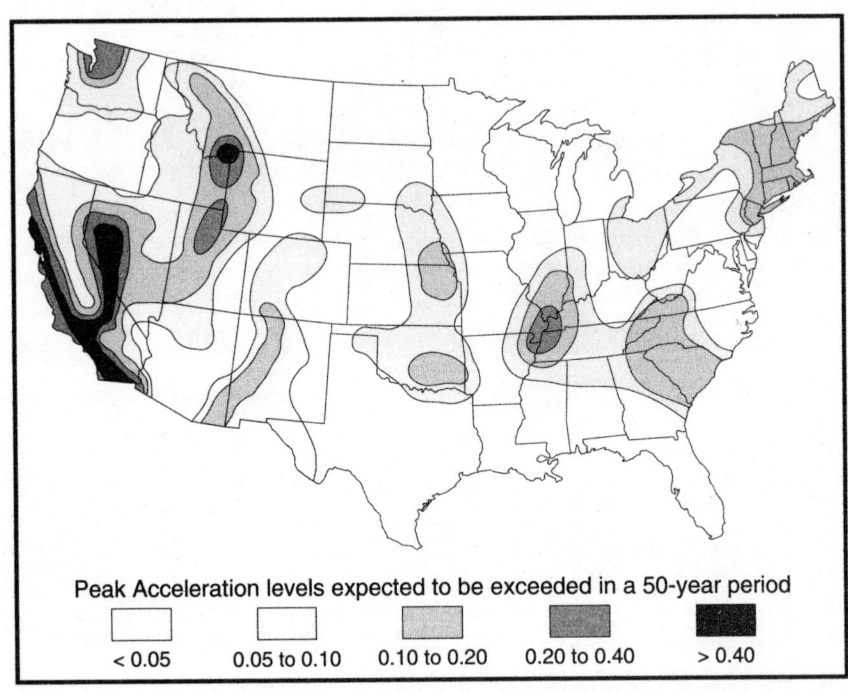

FIGURE 2.1 Distribution of major earthquakes in the United States

Causes of Earthquakes

Historically, there have been many interpretations of causes of earthquakes. In ancient and medieval China, earthquakes were believed to be associated with the natural and human (political) order. Needham (1959:624-5) reports the *Shih Chi*, a first century B.C. comprehensive history of China, as saying:

> It is necessary that the chhi of heaven and earth should not lose their order (pu shih chhi hsu); if they overstep their order (kuo chhi hsu) it is because there is disorder among the people. When the Yang is hidden and cannot come forth, or when the Yin bars its way and it cannot rise up, then there is what we call an earthquake (ti chen).

In Japanese tradition, earthquakes were believed to be caused by the giant *namazu* (catfish) living under the ground (Shoji, 1983).

In Europe, earthquakes were viewed as God's punishment: the 1755 Lisbon earthquake was believed to be divine punishment for the wickedness of the people of the city, or, alternatively, punishment for the Inquisition (Gere and Shah, 1984). Such beliefs have persisted, albeit less commonly; indeed some internet conversation networks report statements by religious leaders calling the 1994 California earthquake a punishment for the wickedness of Los Angelenos.

Plate Tectonics

Today, scientists depend on the theory of plate tectonics to explain the occurrence of earthquakes. This theory postulates that the lithosphere or outermost part of the Earth consists of several large, stable slabs of relatively rigid rock or plates. Plates move horizontally. Where plates contact one another, large forces cause physical or chemical changes. As plates move, they may be buried in the Earth's interior at sites called subduction zones.

This general theory of plate tectonics implies that (1) more earthquakes occur along the edges of interacting plates than within plate boundaries; (2) interplate earthquakes (such as the 1811 New Madrid earthquake) arise from localized forces rather than the interplate forces; (3) most earthquakes occur where plates converge; and (4) a fairly regular pattern of plate movement suggests a recurrent historical pattern of earthquakes with regular distance and time intervals separating the earthquakes along major plate boundaries (Bolt, 1993).

The observation of regular movement at particular time intervals gives credence to the seismic gap model of earthquake prediction: when there has been a below-average release of seismic energy for a period of time, seismologists can predict that a relatively large earthquake will occur to release the accumulated strain. Seismic gap theory is one of the several ways in which future earthquakes are predicted (Bolt, 1993).

Earthquakes thus usually occur on the boundaries of crustal plates--particularly in areas where plates are converging and one plate is being subducted beneath another. Maps of global seismicity show clear patterns of concentrations of earthquakes in arcs, particularly concentrated in the Pacific Rim (Bolt, 1993). However, some of the earthquakes with the largest numbers of associated deaths and destruction, as well as extremely high Richter scale values, occur in inter-plate areas far from plate boundaries (Figure 2.2). Examples are the Tangshan earthquake of 1976 in China, and the three New Madrid earthquakes of 1811 and 1812 in Missouri.

Measures of Damage or Destruction

The seriousness of an earthquake can be measured by its physical magnitude as well as by the amount of damage or loss of life associated with it. A widely used quantitative scale was developed by Charles Richter in 1935. This scale, the Richter scale, measures the amplitudes of waves from a seismograph reading. The magnitude of an earthquake is defined as "the logarithm to base ten of the maximum seismic-wave amplitude (in thousandths of a millimeter) recorded on a standard seismograph at a distance of 100 kilometers from the earthquake epicenter." The Richter scale has been elaborated to adapt it to the use of various seismographs, distances to the epicenter

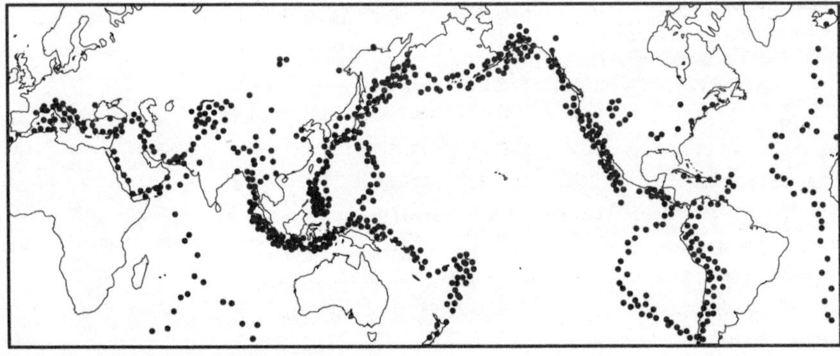

FIGURE 2.2 Major earthquakes in the world

and methods of choosing wave amplitude (whether the P (primary) or S (secondary) wave, for example). The Richter scale is the most common single number used to describe the energy in an earthquake. By Richter scale measurements, very few earthquakes exceed a magnitude of 8.9 (Bolt, 1993).

A more subjective but also more descriptive way of measuring earthquake damage is the use of an intensity scale--a subjective scale indicating the impacts of the event on life, human-made structures, and the surface of the earth. The most commonly used intensity scale is the Modified Mercalli Intensity Scale, created by G. Mercalli and developed by H. O. Wood and Frank Neumann to fit building construction types in California (Bolt, 1993). This scale classifies earthquake damage on a scale of 1 to 12. On this scale, 1 is defined as "not felt except by a few under exceptionally favorable circumstances." Intensity 4 is described as: "during the day felt indoors by many, outdoors by few; at night some awakened. Dishes, windows, doors disturbed; walls make creaking sound. Sensation like heavy truck striking building. Standing automobiles rocked noticeably." At intensity 7, "Everybody runs outdoors. Damage negligible in buildings of good design and construction; slight to moderate in well-built ordinary structures; considerable in poorly built or badly designed structures; some chimneys broke. Noticed by persons driving cars." At the highest intensity of 12, "damage total--waves seen on ground surface, lines of sight and level distorted, objects thrown into the air."

Other ways to indicate the severity of the earthquake are tabulations of loss of life, number of persons suffering serious injury, relative amount of property damage, and extent of disruption to daily life. These measures are very subjective, varying according to the circumstances in which the earthquake takes place.

For example, the death toll from an earthquake of a given magnitude can vary partly as a function of the time of day the earthquake occurs since time-of-day affects the extent to which a population is concentrated in a given work place, commuting, or dispersed in homes. It is even more directly affected by the prevailing type of construction in the area. One reason for the extremely large loss of life associated with the 1556 Shensi China earthquake, with a death toll of more than 800,000, was that a large part of the population lived in caves in unstable *loess* hillsides. The earthquake caused these caves to collapse, crushing and suffocating the victims (Smith, 1992).

A more recent earthquake illustrates the impacts of housing construction-type on loss of life. The 1988 Armenian earthquake (magnitude 6.9) was approximately the same magnitude as the 1989 Loma Prieta earthquake in California. Although the California earthquake claimed 65 lives, the Armenian earthquake resulted in from 25,000 to 100,000 deaths. The Armenian earthquake death toll was so high because victims were crushed inside their own homes, and search and rescue teams were unable to transport survivors promptly to receive medical care and escape from the cold weather. The worst damage occurred at the village of Kirovakan, in a neighborhood where the land had been reclaimed from marshes and the soft sediment amplified the ground motion waves. Older buildings of unreinforced stone masonry cracked and floors collapsed. Newer prefabricated buildings also failed and collapsed. Thus, a moderate magnitude earthquake became translated into a disaster bringing with it large property losses and unnecessarily large loss of life (Wylie and Filson, 1989; Alexander, 1993).

Sources of Damage

At least five sources of potential damage are associated with an earthquake. The primary cause of damage is ground shaking, the violent motion of the ground in the vicinity of the earthquake center, and shaking amplified by soil structure in more distant areas. In the 1989, Loma Prieta earthquake, ground shaking caused about 98 percent of the approximately $6 billion in property damage, while ground deformation (landslides, rupture or liquefaction) accounted for only 2 percent of the damage (Holzer, 1994). A second source of damage is ground rupture, the sudden fracturing of the earth surface. Ground rupture is shown in the dramatic photographs of cracks in the earth following a major earthquake. A third source of damage--fault creep-- is the slow and gradual fracturing of the earth in regions underlain with surface faulting. This source of damage is persistently at work in some areas, causing continuing damage to streets or buildings along the fault traces. A fourth type of earthquake-related damage is ground failure. Depending on the soil structure on which buildings are constructed, ground failure can involve landslides or possibly even liquefaction, the transformation of loose materials such as sand and silt into a fluid-like state resembling quicksand. Liquefaction is a major hazard in areas where land has been reclaimed from bays or estuaries, and major construction has been permitted on loosely packed, fine sands or silts where the water table is close to the ground surface. Numerous areas are subject to liquefaction, including much of the shore surrounding the San Francisco Bay. Finally, another source of damage related to earthquakes is that associated with tsunamis or massive sea waves. These waves (sometimes popularly mislabeled as "tidal waves") may reach heights of 130 feet or more and have caused serious damage in Japan, Hawaii and Alaska.

Earthquake Hazard in California

The phrase "earthquake country" is part of the image of California. Popular books discuss the earthquake problem matter-of-factly: "California is Earthquake Country. Earthquakes are a part of California's heritage and we all must learn to live with them" (Iacopi, 1978:4). The earthquake hazard in California has been recognized from the time of earliest European settlement. For example, Ziony and Kockelman (1985:1) describe the "seismological greeting" to Captain Gaspar de Portola in July 1769 when he and his soldiers arrived in the Los Angeles Basin:

> On the 28th, when the governor and his followers were on the Santa Ana River, four violent shocks of earthquake frightened the Indians into a kind of prayer to the four winds, and caused the stream to be named also Jesus de los Temblores. Many more shocks were felt during the following week; yet the foreigners were delighted with the region, noting the agricultural possibilities.

This selection points up the ambivalence that Europeans settlers as well as contemporary Americans have toward California: a land of promise, a fulfillment of the American Dream (Vance, 1972), but at the same time a place subject to environmental hazards and, recently, to societal risks.

In California, earthquakes are caused by violent motion along the margin of the lithospheric plates: the Pacific or oceanic plate and the North American or continental plate. The San Andreas fault system is the boundary area between these two plates. Slip rates along this fault are from 20 to 30 mm per year (Ziony and Yerkes, 1985). This boundary area passes through several of the state's most densely populated urban regions, including the Los Angeles basin, the San Bernardino region, and the San Francisco Bay area. It is therefore "one of the most extensively urbanized tectonic plate boundaries on Earth" (Yerkes, 1985:25).

Since 1800, California has experienced more than 70 earthquakes of M6 or larger (Orme, 1992). The "great" earthquake of the 20th century was the 1906 San Francisco earthquake that claimed about 2500 lives. Other earthquakes associated with large death tolls and property losses were the Long Beach earthquake of 1933, the San Fernando earthquake of 1971, the Loma Prieta earthquake of 1989, and the Northridge earthquake of 1994 (Figure 2.3).

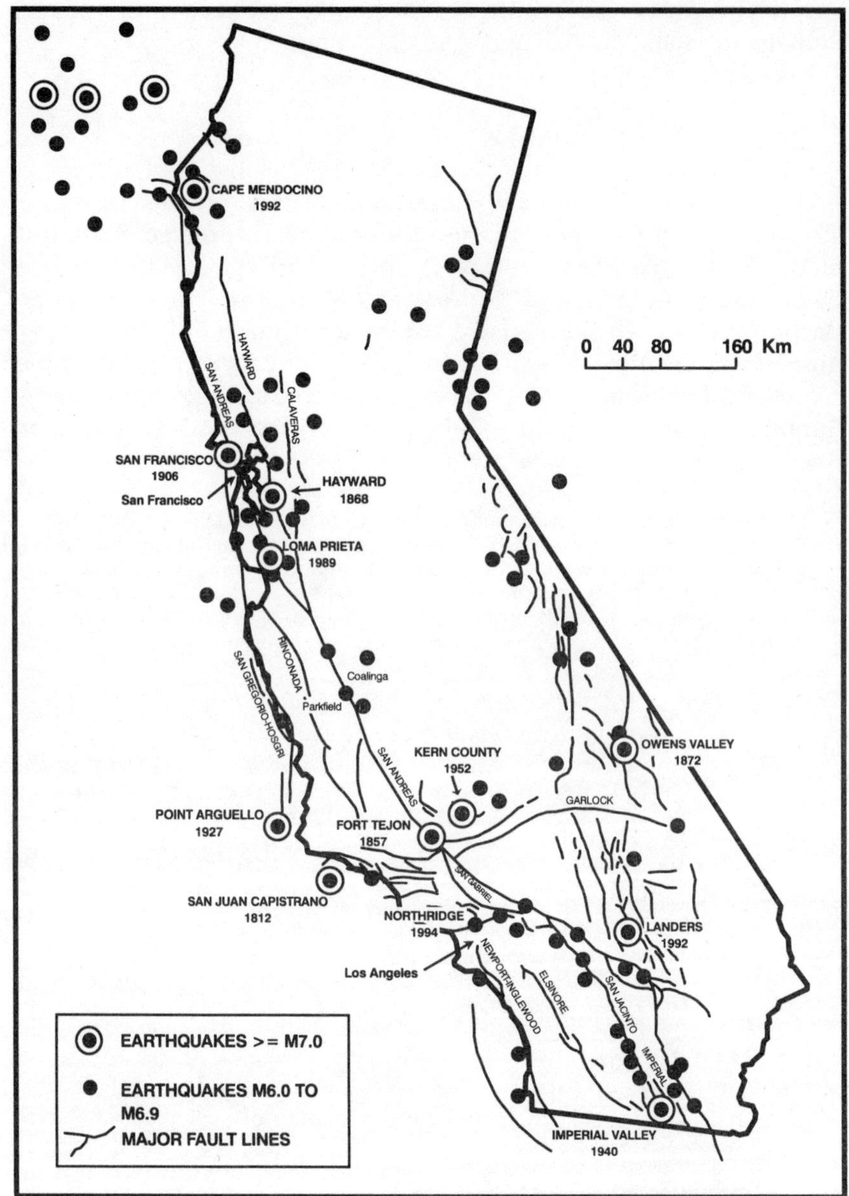

FIGURE 2.3 Major historic earthquakes in California

Much effort has gone into the preparation of planning scenarios to prepare governmental agencies and the general public for probable future earthquakes. The Federal Emergency Management Agency along with the US Geological Survey estimate a high probability (in excess of 40 percent) that a large earthquake will occur within the next thirty years near Los Angeles (Lindh, 1983; Wesson and Wallace, 1985). Projected losses from such an earthquake include as many as 12,500 deaths (Federal Emergency Management Agency, 1980), over 50,000 homeless, and over $25 billion (1980 dollars) in property damage. An earthquake of the magnitude of the Loma Prieta earthquake (in excess of M7) but located along the Hayward fault in the east bay area of the San Francisco region has been estimated with a probability of 67 percent between 1990 and 2020 (Ward, 1990). Such an earthquake would be far more destructive than the recent Loma Prieta or San Fernando earthquakes and would perhaps claim 1500-4500 lives and cause more than $40 billion in damage (Ward and Page, 1990). A smaller magnitude earthquake on the Newport-Inglewood fault, which runs directly through the central business district of Los Angeles, could cause even more death and destruction--21,000 deaths, 200,000 persons homeless and over $60 billion in damage (1980 dollars) (Steinbrugge et al. 1981).

Federal Earthquake Legislation

Federal legislation, like that at state and local levels, is the response to particular seismic events interacting with the agendas of political leaders and lobbying groups. A major federal legislative initiative was stimulated by a combination of the 1964 Alaska earthquake, the 1971 San Fernando earthquake, the 1975-76 earthquake predictions in China and California, as well as by congressional leaders such as Senator Alan Cranston of California. Following the 1964 Alaska earthquake, President Lyndon Johnson directed the National Academy of Sciences to conduct a multidisciplinary study of this earthquake. Both the National Academy of Engineering and the National Academy of Sciences (National Research Council) followed this study with their own broader assessments of earthquake research. The National Academy of Engineering (1969) Committee on Earthquake Engineering report outlines research needs in seismology, engineering and policy issues; the National Research Council report of the same year summarizes lessons to be learned from the Alaska earthquake and calls attention to ways to promote hazard mitigation (Olson et al. 1988; National Research Council, 1969).

The San Fernando earthquake of 1971 further stimulated national attention to the earthquake issue. Again, Senator Alan Cranston introduced bills to expand support for earthquake prediction research (Olson et al. 1988). The Federal Office of Emergency Preparedness initiated a set of activities on earthquake preparedness in 1972, garnering political support for earthquake mitigation programs (Mileti and Fitzpatrick, 1993; Olson et al. 1988).

Finally, publicity surrounding the prediction of earthquakes in China in 1975 and on the southern portion of the San Andreas--the Palmdale Bulge--in 1976 further focused attention on earthquake hazards.

All this activity was brought together in the omnibus Earthquake Hazard Reduction Act of 1977. This federal legislation was the first major national earthquake policy legislation. Its aim was to reduce loss of life and property, by coordinating federal agencies to implement earthquake hazards reduction. This legislation created the National Earthquake Hazards Reduction Program (NEHRP), whose goals were the delineation and assessment of hazards, the encouragement of research into seismic-resistant design and engineering, the development of plans for earthquake preparedness, and promoting an increase in earthquake hazard awareness among the general public. The key agencies were the National Science Foundation, which sponsors basic research and the US Geological Survey, which conducts more applied research. Coordination and leadership for all NEHRP activities are provided by the Federal Emergency Management Agency (FEMA), which links federal with state and local activities. The 1992 summary of federal activity aimed at reducing the impacts of natural hazards (Committee on Earthquake and Environmental Sciences, 1992:79) characterizes the role of FEMA as follows:

> The National Earthquake Hazards Reduction Program, in which FEMA, together with USGS, NIST, and NSF provides to State and local governments the materials and assistance needed to educate citizens living in earthquake-prone areas about earthquake hazards, the technical guidance and assistance for erecting seismic-resistant buildings and implementing other mitigation procedures, and the training and information for preparedness, response and recovery from earthquakes.

Thus, federal legislation, beginning as a stimulus to research, has evolved into a comprehensive and multidisciplinary program spanning several agencies and attempting not only to understand the basic science of seismology and the applied science of earthquake engineering, but also to prepare local entities and citizens to adopt mitigation measures and respond to disaster events in ways that will reduce death, injuries and financial losses.

California Earthquake Legislation

Legislation in California, at both the state and local level, has attempted to regulate the private development of property and the employment of construction techniques. It has also aimed at providing information to the general public about earthquake risks and possible mitigation responses. Legislation in California has been enacted with increasing frequency, particularly in the immediate post-disaster environment.

The first evidence of official state involvement in earthquake hazards was the reprinting of the 1888 eighth annual report of the state mineralogist that described the Owens Valley earthquake of 1872 (Joint Committee on Seismic Safety, 1974). After the 1906 earthquake, the governor appointed a state earthquake investigation commission which published a two-volume report and atlas of the earthquake. After the Long Beach earthquake of 1933, the state legislature passed the Field Act mandating that the State Office of Architecture and Construction set up rules and regulations concerning earthquake safety in the design and construction of school buildings. There was a considerable lull in activity until the 1964 earthquake in Anchorage, Alaska. This earthquake stimulated the establishment of the Joint Committee on Seismic Safety in 1969, which was chartered to compile information on structural engineering, geological and seismological conditions, land-use planning, disaster preparedness, and the organization of government to cope with disaster.

The San Fernando earthquake of 1971 was followed by renewed legislative activity. New legislation included the Special Studies Zone Act, the Hospital Seismic Safety Act, the Strong Motion Instrumentation Act, the evaluation of earthquake-vulnerable dams, the preparation of inundation maps and plans for downstream evacuation, and plans to retrofit highway bridges (Tobin, 1988). At the county and city level, all general plans were henceforth to contain a seismic safety element, including the identification and appraisal of seismic hazards.

The Coalinga earthquake of 1983, reinforced by the devastating earthquake in Mexico City in 1985, further stimulated state legislation (Tobin, 1988). The Earthquake Hazards Reduction Act of 1985, state standards for essential service facilities (1985), and an act requiring an inventory of unreinforced masonry buildings (1986) were all passed during this period. Local jurisdictions enacted legislation regulating unreinforced masonry buildings. Earthquake insurance disclosure legislation was passed during this time, requiring that insurance companies disclose the availability of earthquake insurance to homeowners' insurance policy-holders. A prototype earthquake prediction system including a comprehensive emergency response plan was set up for the Parkfield section of the San Andreas fault.

In virtually every case, legislation was developed in response to some immediate crisis, such as an earthquake in California or elsewhere demonstrating the destructive capability of such events. In addition, key individuals had a great impact in both promoting and opposing particular pieces of legislation. Alesch and Petak (1986) report several examples of the negotiations involved in legislative activity. For example, legislation that would have required building rehabilitation to increase seismic safety to older motion picture theaters was opposed by the Association of Motion Picture and Television Producers on the grounds that such regulations would put undue financial burdens on the industry. The Society of Theater Historians joined this battle on the grounds that such theaters were part of the "Los Angeles cultural heritage" and therefore should be preserved in their current condition (Alesch and Petak, 1986:58-59). At the same time, individuals in the state legislature, in city government, and outside of government promoted legislation that would increase seismic safety and increase the dissemination of information about earthquake risk.

Public Information

All efforts at the federal, state and local levels aim, at least in part, at increasing public awareness of the earthquake hazard. Do Californians have sufficient information to make decisions about the adoption of mitigation measures? Recent research indicates (Mileti and Fitzpatrick, 1993:86) that people will take action when they as individuals are motivated to search for information and define the kinds of tasks they need to undertake: "all readiness activities were mostly the consequence of having engaged in their own search for more information . . . The search actually reflected people's needs to interact with other people and to talk things over. This was the way people formed personal definitions about the risks they faced as individuals and about actions they should perform." But what motivates this search? Mileti and Fitzpatrick answer that the motivation "evolved over time and was the result of information being heard over and over again from varied sources and over different channels of communication." They found that a brochure presenting "information that was comprehensive, specific, clear, consistent, credible and accurate" was the most effective means of convincing individuals to take action.

What kinds of information are available to Californians about the earthquake hazard and about insurance as a remedy? Public information about earthquake hazards is disseminated through a large and growing number of sources. Teacher training programs introduce earthquake mitigation units into the public schools (Thier, 1988). Scout organizations have earthquake mitigation badges. Local governments sponsor earthquake awareness days. For example, the City of Los Angeles, assisted by Universal Studios, developed footage of a simulated Los Angeles earthquake (Mattingly, 1987). Street atlases contain overlays showing Special Studies Zones (surface fault rupture zones). Telephone books contain information on emergency procedures to follow during an earthquake. Since 1976, real estate agents are required to disclose locations within a surface fault rupture zone as part of the Alquist-Priolo Special Studies Zones act (Figure 2.4). Later amendments to this legislation now require real estate agents to present to buyers of all homes built before 1960 copies of "The Homeowner's Guide to Earthquake Safety," a booklet containing information on geologic and seismic hazards and recommendations for mitigating the hazards (Business and Professions Code, Article 1, Chapter 3, Sections 10130-10149). This booklet is also available to the general public (Civil Code, Section 2079.8). The US Geological Survey, the Office of the State Geologist, the Federal Emergency Management Agency, SCEPP, BAREPP, BICEPP, and other organizations develop and distribute brochures, maps, scientific reports and other materials on the earthquake hazard and measures that can be adopted to mitigate some of its effects. The *Los Angeles Times* has published maps and reports on earthquake hazards. On September 9, 1990, the major Bay Area newspapers including the *San Jose Mercury* and the *San Francisco Chronicle* published a 24 page four-color insert entitled, "The Next Big Earthquake in the Bay Area May Come Sooner than You Think." This insert describes revised predictions for an earthquake in the Bay Area and measures the public can undertake to respond to such an earthquake. Mileti and Fitzpatrick (1993:92) describe the development and publication of this insert as representing "perhaps for the first time in the history of the nation, the cooperation of federal, state, local and private-sector organizations as well as the blending of social scientific knowledge about communicating risk information to the public with what the physical scientists had to say."

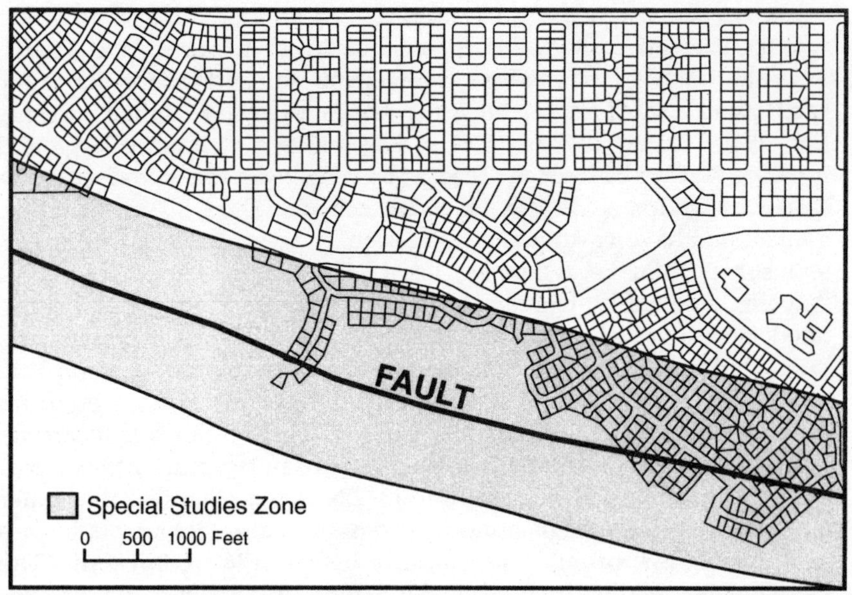

FIGURE 2.4 Special studies zones

In short, public information about the earthquake hazard and recommended steps to prepare for an earthquake is widespread. The remaining question is whether people attend to this information and even more importantly, whether this information spurs people to action.

Summary

California is not unique in its exposure to earthquake hazards. However, because of the concentration of population in areas subject to frequent earthquakes, it is probably the area within the United States most vulnerable to damage and destruction. A series of federal and state laws have stimulated research into both the physical processes triggering earthquakes and the social scientific aspects of risk communication and hazard mitigation adoption. State-level legislation in California has made detailed information about the earthquake hazard and the availability of insurance widely accessible. In the following chapters, we will explore the extent to which California homeowners have acted on this information to adopt insurance or other measures that would make their homes and their property less vulnerable to earthquake-related damage.

3

Earthquake Hazard Mitigation: The Role of Insurance

California residents are at extreme risk of losing lives and sustaining injuries as a consequence of earthquakes. Furthermore, billions of dollars of residential property in California is susceptible to damage or loss from earthquakes. Although insuring property will not save lives or prevent injuries, it can reduce some of the financial consequences of earthquakes for individual households. The purpose of this chapter is to describe earthquake insurance as a mitigation strategy.

What is property insurance? This form of insurance reduces financial losses to property owners from fire or other catastrophes, as well as protecting the homeowner from financial losses associated with the possibility that someone may be injured while on the property and hold the owner liable. The first standardized fire insurance policy was developed in 1886 in the state of New York. This fire insurance policy is the basis for other property damage insurance written in the United States (Harwood and Jacobus, 1990: 518).

In addition to fire, other causes of property loss include hail, tornado, earthquake, riot, windstorm, smoke damage, explosion, glass breakage, landslide, ground failure, subsidence, water pipe leaks, vandalism, freezing and building collapse. The basic homeowners' insurance coverage policy (HO-1) covers damage from fire or lightning, losses sustained while removing property from an endangered premises, windstorm or hail damage, explosion, riot or commotion, aircraft, vehicles, smoke, vandalism and malicious mischief, theft, and breakage of glass that is part of the building. In addition, a broad coverage policy (HO-2) adds coverage from falling objects, weight of ice, snow and sleet, collapse of the building, sudden and accidental cracking, burning or bulging of a steam or hot water heating system or of appliances for heating water, freezing of plumbing, heating and air conditional systems and domestic appliances, and sudden and accidental injury from artificially generated currents to electrical appliances, devices, fixtures and wiring. Excluded from such coverage is damage from flood, landslide, mud flow, tidal wave, earthquake, underground water, settling, cracking, war and nuclear accident.

Since 1968, insurance for flood hazard has been available at subsidized rates for those within the hundred-year flood plain in communities that are part of the National Flood Insurance program. Property owners may be covered from damage caused by overflow of inland or tidal waters, unusual or rapid accumulation or runoff of surface waters, mud slides resulting from accumulation of water, and erosion losses caused by abnormal water runoff. Mortgages involving the federal government require a certificate that the mortgaged property is not in a flood zone or that the property is covered by flood insurance.

Earthquake damage is not covered by either the basic or broad coverage. However, separate earthquake insurance can be added as an endorsement to the homeowner's insurance policy. The focus of this chapter is the circumstances under which homeowners decide to add this type of coverage. For people to elect to purchase earthquake insurance, they must know that it is available and decide that the cost of the premiums is not prohibitively high for the benefit of coverage.

Cost of Insurance

To decide whether to buy earthquake insurance, homeowners need to know how much insurance costs and what the estimated benefits of purchasing insurance are. Costs of insurance include two components: the premium and the deductible. The premium is the annual payment the individual makes for a given level of insurance. The deductible is the proportion of the loss that the insured party must pay as opposed to that paid by the insurance company. Premiums and deductibles are determined by the insurance rate zone in which the county of residence is located and the type of home construction. California includes three rate zones: most of urban California including the San Francisco Bay Area, Los Angeles, San Diego and San Bernardino-Riverside is in the highest rate zone. Within a given zone, the least expensive premiums are paid by owners of small, wood-frame structures with three or fewer stories. Highest premiums are paid for buildings of unreinforced adobe, hollow clay tile or unreinforced hollow concrete block.

In the highest risk areas of California, coverage for wood-frame residential dwellings (the most common type of construction) costs about $2.00 to $2.50 per $1,000 of coverage with a 10 percent deductible. For example, the owner of a $300,000 property with $200,000 insurance on the house would pay an annual premium of $400 to $500. With a 10 percent deductible, the first $20,000 in loss to the structure would be deducted from any claim.

The financial benefits of insurance are more difficult to calculate. Some estimate that in a probable earthquake, the amount of damage to a single-family wood-frame home is unlikely to exceed 10 percent of its value: the damage would not be much greater than the deductible on the policy, resulting in no collection on damage claims. In recent history, however, immense insurance claims have resulted after only moderate-strength earthquakes. The estimated probability of such an event occurring at a given property should thus be the key ingredient in the individual earthquake purchase decision.

Availability of Earthquake Insurance

Earthquake insurance has been available since 1916 and may be purchased simply as an addendum to fire insurance policies. As mandated by state law, it is available from all companies that sell other homeowner's insurance in California. It may be purchased at any time except for a short moratorium period immediately after an earthquake.

Recent California state legislation promotes awareness of the availability of earthquake insurance. This legislation evolved from a set of legal interpretations protecting both the insurers and the insured (Brown, 1987). The Superior Court of Marin County, California, in its Garvey decision established the principle of concurrent causation: when two or more causes combine to produce a loss and when one of those causes is not excluded from insurance coverage, the loss is covered. This decision meant that if an earthquake combined with poor construction causes structural damage, then damage from the earthquake would be covered by the existing homeowner's policy.

As a result of extensive lobbying by the insurance industry, state legislation insulating insurance companies from this type of claim went into effect in January 1985. In exchange for protection from concurrent causation liability, the insurers had to offer homeowner's insurance policy-holders the opportunity to buy earthquake insurance. The 1984 California legislation states that "it is the intent of the Legislature in enacting this act to promote awareness of earthquake insurance by residential property owners and tenants by requiring insurers to offer that coverage" (§1081, Section 2 of Stats. 1984, c. 916.

California Insurance Code). Thus, insurers in California are required to offer earthquake insurance as a condition for continuing to offer homeowner's insurance in the state.

In addition to specifying that insurers must offer earthquake insurance, the legislation states that an offer must be made by certified mail to demonstrate a conclusive presumption that it is voluntarily declined. The statute requires that the insurance company's offer contain the following language:

> Your policy does not provide coverage against the peril of earthquake. California law requires that earthquake coverage be offered to you at your option. The coverage, subject to policy provisions, may be purchased at additional cost on the following terms: (a) amount of the coverage: ___; (b) applicable deductible: ____; (c) rate or premium: _____. You must ask the company to add earthquake coverage within 30 days from the date of mailing of this notice or it shall be conclusively presumed that you have not accepted this offer. This coverage shall be effective on the day your acceptance of this offer is received by us.

This offer of earthquake insurance must be made prior to, concurrent with, or within 60 days following the issuance or renewal of a residential property insurance policy. The offer is renewed each time the policy is renewed.

The 1984 legislation is extremely important in making earthquake insurance widely available and in making this availability known to prospective purchasers. This legislation ensures that information about the availability of earthquake insurance is provided to everyone who also carries homeowner's insurance. Clearly, any argument of lack of availability is misplaced; people may choose not to buy earthquake insurance, but their decision is not related to its availability.

Insuring the Deductible

Additional state legislation went into effect for the 1992 calendar year: the California Residential Earthquake Recovery Fund was passed in 1990 and was in effect by January, 1992. This fund provided for mandatory insurance of up to $15,000 to cover losses associated with the deductible on catastrophic insurance. This coverage was required of all homeowners whether or not they chose to purchase catastrophic earthquake insurance.

The legislation establishing this fund evolved directly from experience with the Loma Prieta earthquake. This earthquake demonstrated to homeowners the negative financial impacts of a 10 percent deductible on their personal losses (Roth, 1990). The result was pressure from homeowners for basic protection up to $15,000 with a small deductible, a coverage that the private insurance industry did not feel they could afford.to provide (Roth, 1990).

The 1992 state program levied a surcharge of from $12 to $60 (depending on location and type of dwelling) on residential and mobile home insurance policies. These surcharges were collected by the insurance companies but sent to the California State Treasury to be placed in an account free of federal or state taxation. The program provided coverage up to $15,000 for the structure only, subject to deductibles of $1,000 to $3,500 (depending on the value of the house).

In the absence of this policy, insured homeowners usually had to pay 10 percent of the losses themselves, with the insurance company paying the balance. These proportions meant that with a 10 percent deductible, a $50,000 loss on a $400,000 home (not unusual in the Loma Prieta earthquake) would cost the insured homeowner $40,000 and the insurance company $10,000. For a $100,000 loss, the insurance company would pay $60,000 while the homeowner paid the same $40,000.

The state program changed the division of losses paid by the insurance company and the homeowner. For example, the owner of a $200,000 home suffering a $40,000 loss would pay $6,000 and the state of California would pay $14,000. If the homeowner was insured, the insurance company would pay the remaining $20,000. If the homeowner was uninsured, he would pay the remaining $20,000, or a total of $26,000.

Despite the program's popular appeal, it was repealed in September 1992, effective January 1, 1993. The program was thus in effect for only the calendar year 1992. An estimated 90 percent of California homeowners paid the surcharge for this program (personal communication, Richard Roth and Bill Gage, September 1992).

Publicity surrounding this legislation may have increased public awareness of earthquake insurance. In addition, the experience of paying a premium for a small amount of earthquake coverage may have made the public more aware of the utility of catastrophic earthquake insurance as an economic protection against the impacts of major damaging earthquakes. The possible effects of this experience with a form of publicly-provided insurance on the propensity to purchase private catastrophic insurance was part of the question that the 1993 survey addressed.

Conclusion

Earthquake insurance is an important economic measure that the household can adopt to prevent some of the devastating economic consequences of an earthquake. It is widely available, except during a short moratorium on purchase immediately after a major earthquake. Various legislative strategies have increased the probability that individuals are aware of its existence and cost. Several recent state bills may have increased the likelihood that homeowners would purchase insurance. These include bills requiring greater provision of information about earthquake risk and potential mitigation measures in situ, disclosure of information concerning the availability and cost of insurance, and the 1992 experience with a small mandatory insurance policy. In the next chapters, we will explore the effects of these policies on perceived vulnerability and the adoption of hazard mitigation measures including insurance purchase.

4

The 1993 Study

The study reported in this book is the third survey of what was originally a randomly selected sample of owner-occupiers in four California counties: Contra Costa, Santa Clara, Los Angeles and San Bernardino. The purpose of this survey is to assess trends in earthquake insurance adoption, changes in attitudes toward earthquake risk, trends in the adoption of mitigation measures, and factors associated with changes in these attitudes and behaviors. In this chapter, the nature of the survey is described.

The Study Areas

The four counties in this survey were selected to represent vulnerable portions of urban areas in both northern and southern California (Figure 4.1). The four counties, all of which are transected by active surface fault traces, represent a diversity of socioeconomic and demographic characteristics and settlement histories (Table 4.1).

Contra Costa County is part of the San Francisco metropolitan area and contains suburbs from which a large middle-class population commutes to the business districts of Oakland and San Francisco daily via automobile or BART (Bay Area Rapid Transit). With almost a million residents in 1990, its population is typical of a suburban county: more than a third of the employed population is professional-managerial, almost two-thirds of the housing is owner-occupied and more than two-thirds of the housing stock has been built since 1960. The county has a relatively low percentage of families below the poverty level (5.5 percent) and contains an industrial area used for oil refining and other port-oriented activities. The county is transected by the Calaveras and Concord faults, running through the suburban areas of Dublin, Danville, Alamo, Walnut Creek, Concord, Pleasant Hill

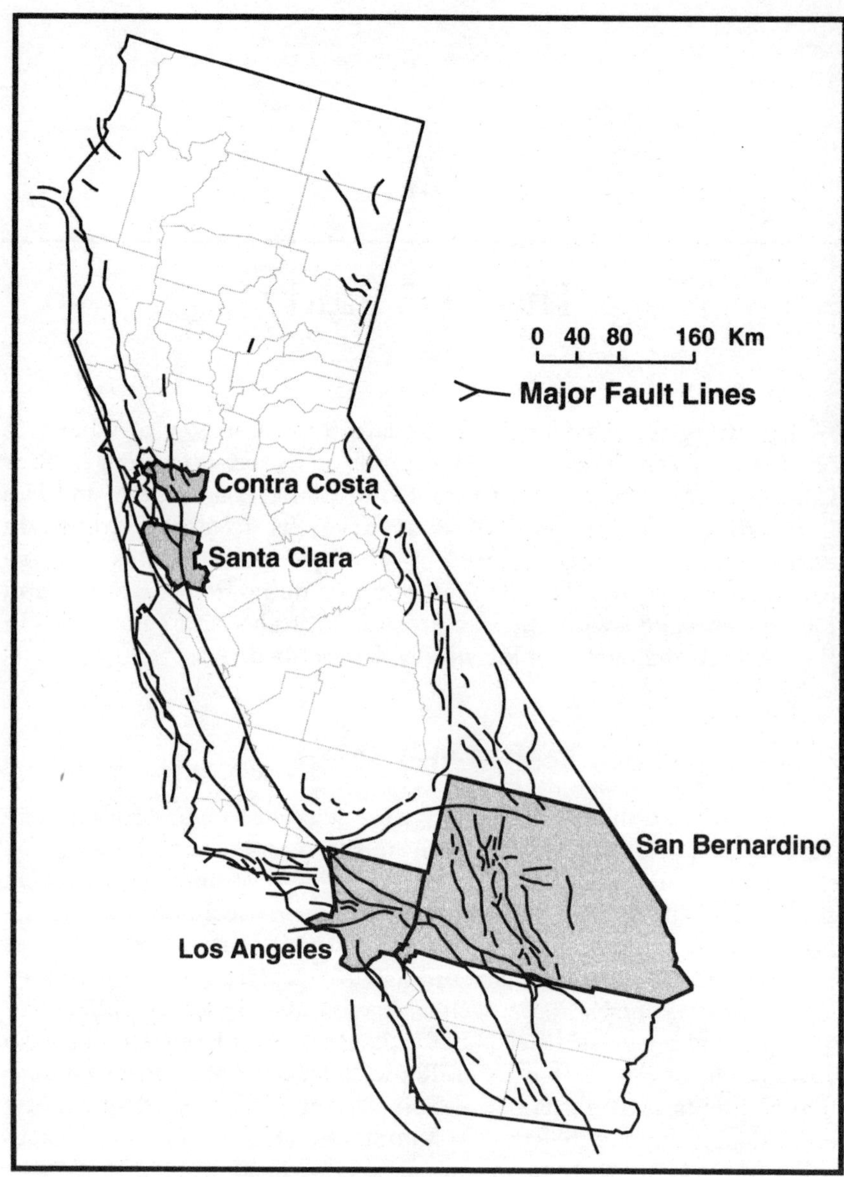

FIGURE 4.1 California study counties

and Martinez, and is also crossed by the Hayward fault in industrial Richmond, San Pablo and Pinole.

TABLE 4.1 1990 Census Information on the Four Study Counties

	Contra Costa	Santa Clara	Los Angeles	San Bernardino	All California
Population (in thousands)					
1970	556. 1	1,065.3	7,041.9	682.2	19,972.2
1980	656.3	1,295.1	7,477.2	895.0	23,667.8
1990	803.7	1,497.6	8,863.1	1,418.4	29,760.0
Median family income	51,651	53,670	39,035	36,997	50,559
Percent prof/managerial	34.3	35.0	27.6	23.8	28.6
Percent families below poverty level	5.5	5.0	11.6	10.3	9.3
Percent non-white	24.0	31.1	43.2	27.0	31.0
Percent African -American	9.3	3.8	11.2	8.1	7.4
Percent Asian	9.3	17.0	10.4	3.9	9.2
Percent Hispanic	11.4	21.0	37.8	26.7	25.8
Percent housing owner-occupied	64.1	56.9	45.5	54.3	51.6
Housing built since 1960	67.6	69.8	49.3	74.7	62.9

Santa Clara County was formerly a major fruit and nut producing agricultural region. It is now home of the major city of San Jose and the smaller suburbs of Los Gatos, Los Altos, Sunnyvale, Mountain View, and Palo Alto. Parts of the area are referred to as the Silicon Valley. This county is the wealthiest of the study counties, with more than a third of the employed residents engaged in professional-managerial occupations and a median family income exceeding $53,000 in 1990 (compared to a state average of $40,000). The percentage of non-white population is identical to that of the state as a whole, with a very large fraction of the non-white population being Asian in origin. Almost 70 percent of the housing has been built since 1960. The epicenter of the 1989 Loma Prieta earthquake was in Santa Cruz County, just a few miles from the boundary with Santa Clara County. Major damage occurred within the county as a result of this earthquake. The urbanized portion of the county lies between two major, active faults, the San Andreas fault to the west and the Hayward fault to the east. These two faults converge in the small agricultural town of Hollister.

Los Angeles County is the most heavily populated of the study counties with almost 9 million residents according to the 1990 census. It is also the most economically and ethnically diverse. It has the oldest housing stock, with more than 50 percent built before 1960, the largest fraction of non-owner-occupied housing (54.5 percent), the largest fraction of non-white, black, and Hispanic population, and the largest percentage of families below the poverty level. Los Angeles County also contains communities, such as Beverly Hills, with some of the highest income levels in the nation and with single-family housing values often exceeding $5 million. Major faults within the county include the Newport-Inglewood running through the central business district of Los Angeles, and also the San Fernando, the San Gabriel and the San Andreas faults.

The fourth study area was San Bernardino County, an independent metropolitan area within southern California. The county contains both older agricultural and mining towns, and newer suburbs and retirement communities. The housing stock is relatively new (three-fourths constructed since 1960), but the county contains very large percentages of poor families (over 10 percent of the households below the poverty level, exceeding the average rate for all of California), and a high fraction of Hispanic residents (more than one-fourth). The county is also below-average in the percentage of professional-managerial workers. This county has been the site of major earthquakes, including the 1992 Landers quake. Both the San Andreas and the San Jacinto faults run through the more densely populated portion of the county.

Survey Sample

The original sample, first surveyed in 1989, was limited to owner-occupiers. Condominium dwellers were excluded because of our focus on the insurance purchase decision: in the condominium, the decision to purchase insurance is made by a collectivity such as a homeowners' association, involving group negotiations and interactions beyond the scope of the study. Renters were not included in the sample because we focused on protection of the structure as well as the contents in the insurance/mitigation decision process. We decided to survey only those owners who actually occupied the premises in order to link risk perception with actual geophysical risk at the site.

Owner-occupiers, of course, are not the population most vulnerable to the harmful effects of earthquakes: instead, it is those with the least resources, living in housing that is old and has not been brought up to code, who are more likely to suffer damage, injury and even death in the event of an earthquake. For these less wealthy families, the financial losses associated with an earthquake can result in collapse of their daily lives and long-term economic prospects. These families are least likely to be able to afford to prepare for the earthquake--to store, food, water, and emergency supplies to survive the first 72 hours--and cannot afford extraordinary expensive private medical care and highly priced emergency supplies following the disaster.

Although the population of owner-occupiers is not at greatest peril, the responses of this population hold considerable interest. This population is in a financial position to have assets at risk. Also, since this population has sufficient household resources to respond to environmental risk, the intervening variable of severe resource constraints becomes less significant in the decision to adopt mitigation measures including insurance. For these reasons, owner-occupiers are an ideal population in which to study relatively unconstrained decision-making in face of a hazardous environment.

Cross-Sectional Study Population

The 1993 survey involves two overlapping study populations, one cross-sectional and the other longitudinal. The cross-sectional study is an analysis of a sample of households at locations randomly selected in 1989 and surveyed in 1989, 1990 and 1993. The responses from this set of surveys can be considered representative of the owner-occupiers in the four study counties in 1989, and only slightly less representative in the subsequent years.

The original sample included approximately 3500 households in the four counties. Of these 3500 households, a total of 1512 were re-surveyed in 1990. By 1993, because of either non-response to one of the first two surveys or attrition resulting from change in the household (moving, divorce, death, and so forth), only 1000 of the original households remained available for the third survey. Further, we were uncertain as to whether the same individual in the household responded to both the first and second survey. We therefore bifurcated the survey population for the purpose of the third (1993) survey.

For addresses from which we received no returned questionnaire in the first or second survey, we re-checked the name of the current owner-occupier. If the name was the same as the 1989 list, we used that name. If the name of the owner had changed by 1993, we used the new name in the mailing list. We then sent questionnaires to all of these individuals on the updated mailing list. The responses from this set of individuals were used in the cross-sectional comparisons of county-level shifts in attitudes and behavior over the period of the study.

Longitudinal Study Population

For all those who had responded to both the first and second survey, we sent the third survey, asking the respondents to indicate whether they had "personally responded to a similar survey from us in 1989" and also had responded in 1990. The responses of those who said "yes" to both questions, who testified that they personally had responded in 1989 and 1990 as well as in 1993, were used in the longitudinal analysis testing for changes in attitudes and behaviors of individuals. Responses from some of the respondents who claimed that they had responded in both years, but whose demographic characteristics (age, for example) did not fit the respondent profile in 1989 were deleted from this analysis. Because of survey attrition and our desire to be scrupulously accurate in recording repeated responses only from the same individuals, this sample is small and no longer a random sample of owner-occupiers in the county. It does, however, provide longitudinal information on which we can analyze change in attitude and behavior in the same individuals.

The primary advantage of longitudinal research--and particularly panel studies that re-survey the same population--is that the research can trace a complex process by studying changes in specific individuals (Hujer and Schneider, 1989; Bjorklund, 1989; Klevmarken, 1989; Ashenfelter and Solon, 1982; Andrisani, 1980; Sontag, 1971; Schaie, 1983; Morgan et al. 1974; Hagenaars, 1990; Mumford, Stokes and Owens, 1990; Warwick and Lininger, 1975). This technique has immense methodological advantages over a series of cross-sectional studies in its ability to chart change and identify process.

One disadvantage in using panel studies is the reinterview effect or the test-retest effect. Answering a questionnaire may in itself have an impact on the beliefs or the behavior of the individual: the individual learns from the questionnaire, and therefore by the second round is no longer representative of the population from which he/she was drawn. Although we recognize that this effect is a practical problem of this mode of inquiry, the negative or distorting impacts of this effect seem to be minimal. As Hagenaars (1990: 263-4) argues, "Usually no large effects are found. . . . Especially when several months or years lie between the interviews, being interviewed for one or two hours is most probably not such an influential event in the life of a respondent that serious test-retests have to be expected." Given the barrage of information affecting individuals in California about the hazards of earthquakes as well as other problems of daily life, we expected that the earlier questionnaires had minimal or negligible influence on attitude or behavior.

A more serious disadvantage of the longitudinal study is panel attrition--losing participants for various reasons at subsequent stages of the study. This set of studies did indeed experience a high rate of attrition over the period of 1989 to 1993. Nonetheless, we proceeded with this longitudinal data gathering because of the advantages of charting changes in attitudes and behaviors for the same individuals over a longer period of time.

Survey Method

The cross-sectional survey sample was drawn from county lists of taxpayers in 1989. These records are updated each year for property improvements, land use changes, and property transactions. The record contains the names and addresses for all properties on the tax roll in each county. A random sample of approximately 1000 names from each county was drawn from this list. The addresses were then geocoded--that is, assigned a latitude and longitude position. This geocoding was done by the county geographic information system centers for Santa Clara and Los Angeles counties, and by Geobase, a private contractor, for San Bernardino and Contra Costa counties. Only names that could be geocoded were used in the final sampling process, resulting in a reduction from the original 4000 to approximately 3500 in the 1989 sample list.

Three surveys were conducted, in 1989, 1990 and 1993. The first survey was undertaken to update the findings of a large-scale survey of flood and earthquake insurance in 1973-74 by the Kunreuther team (Kunreuther et al. 1978). Five events that took place since the Kunreuther survey are particularly relevant to a change in insurance purchase: (1) the implementation of the Alquist-Priolo Special Studies Zone Act of 1972 requiring the disclosure of location within a surface fault rupture zone to all prospective home buyers; (2) the Coalinga earthquake of 1983 with accompanying publicity about earthquake vulnerability; (3) a barrage of public information campaigns from state and local government as well as private enterprise; (4) increasing interest by the insurance industry in fiscal problems associated with the potential destruction of insured property from a major earthquake, culminating in the creation of a coalition of insurance companies in the Earthquake Project and the attempt to pass federal legislation creating a federal reinsurance program; and (5) the passage of legislation in 1985 mandating that insurance companies doing business in California disclose the availability of earthquake insurance (Figure 4.2). The first survey was completed over the spring and summer of 1989.

A second survey was conducted in summer 1990. This survey was triggered by the Loma Prieta earthquake on October 17, 1989. This magnitude 7.1 earthquake with an epicenter 16 km northeast of Santa Cruz was one of the strongest to occur in California since 1906. Buildings were damaged in San Francisco, Marin, Alameda, San Mateo, Santa Cruz and Santa Clara counties. In addition, severe damage occurred to the Nimitz Freeway (Interstate 880), the San Francisco-Oakland Bay Bridge and Highway 480 (the Embarcadero Freeway), tangling commuter traffic for several months after the earthquake.

Two counties included in the 1989 survey suffered direct impacts from the Loma Prieta earthquake. Santa Clara County was at the heart of the area strongly affected by the earthquake. Residents of Contra Costa County who regularly commuted to San Francisco suffered disruptions in their daily schedules. The two southern California counties experienced the earthquake only indirectly--through stories in local media or communications from friends and relatives living in the Bay Area. These different levels of experience with an earthquake made this recently surveyed population an unusual field

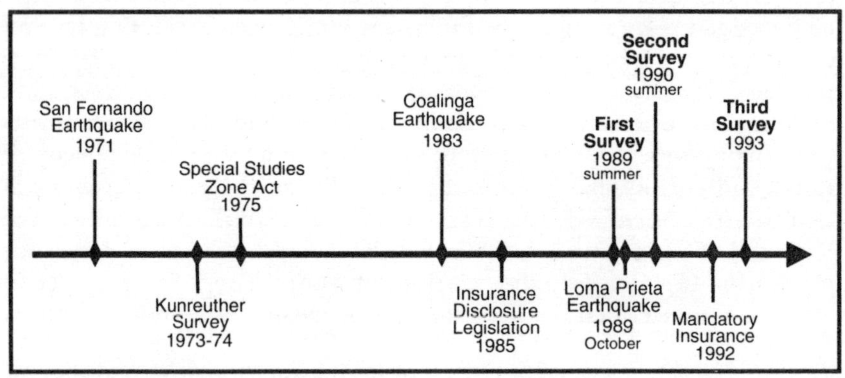

FIGURE 4.2 Timing of surveys

design to test for the impacts of varying levels of experience with an earthquake on the insurance purchase decisions, perceived risk and the adoption of non-insurance mitigation measures.

The third survey, which is the focus of this book, was undertaken in early 1993. The impetus for this survey was the passage in 1990 of a mandatory quasi-insurance policy that would cover small losses with a very low deductible. This program, the California Residential Earthquake Recovery Fund, was passed in 1990 and was in effect only during the 1992 calendar year. This legislation provided mandatory insurance of up to $15,000 to cover losses associated with the deductible on catastrophic insurance.

The legislation providing deductible coverage emanated from experience with the Loma Prieta earthquake. This earthquake demonstrated to homeowners the consequences of a 10 percent deductible on their personal losses. As Roth (1990: 833) relates it, "Even though 30-35 percent of the homes had earthquake coverage, the deductible was 10 percent of the coverage, which often amounted to $20,000. A large number of people protested to their insurers and to the Legislature. People also protested over the 10 percent deductible after the Whittier earthquake." Although the industry had adopted a 10 percent deductible to reduce their risk in moderate earthquakes and therefore insure more homes with the same amount of capital, the 10 percent deductible became politically insupportable. Homeowners pressured for basic protection up to $15,000, a coverage that the insurance industry did not want to provide (Roth, 1990: 833).

The new legislation reduced the costs of small losses to homeowners; however, it did not address the risk of truly catastrophic losses. Indeed, the bill itself states, "The Legislature recognizes that the California Residential Earthquake Recovery Fund is not a substitute for the purchase of private insurance (Section 50121)," and Assistant Insurance Commissioner Richard Roth testified to Congress that the California legislature "supports both private earthquake insurance and federal efforts" (Roth, 1990:833).

The 1993 study tested the hypothesis that the new insurance requirement would cause an increase in catastrophic insurance purchase. Those who already had catastrophic insurance and were required to buy additional insurance on the deductible were expected to strengthen their expectations of a major damaging earthquake affecting their own homes, and maintain their catastrophic insurance policies .

The 1993 survey repeated some of the questions on the 1989 and 1990 surveys to elicit information on (1) perceived probability of a major damaging earthquake and estimates of associated losses, and (2) demographic characteristics of the household (number of resident dependents, age of the head of household, length of time the household has had earthquake insurance, length of time of residence in the region and in the house). Additional questions probed responses to the new mandatory earthquake insurance.

Response Rate and Mode of Analysis

The Total Design Method (Dillman, 1978) was employed for the mail survey. This method involves a sequence of mailings designed to increase the response rate. The sequence includes four steps: (1) the initial mailing of a cover letter and questionnaire; (2) seven days later, a postcard thanking respondents and reminding nonrespondents to return their questionnaires; (3) 21 days after the initial mailing, a letter and a second questionnaire to the nonrespondents; and (4) 49 days after the initial mailing, a letter and replacement questionnaire sent by certified mail to nonrespondents. Each step increases the cumulative response rate.

The response rate for the 1993 cross-sectional survey exceeded 50 percent for all counties and was above 67 percent in Santa Clara County (Table 4.2). This response rate is somewhat lower than the 1990 response rates of 71 percent (Contra Costa), 74 percent (Santa Clara), 65 percent (Los Angeles) and 64 percent (San Bernardino).

In contrast, there was a very high rate of attrition in the longitudinal survey. Very few of the original respondents said that they remembered answering all three surveys. The "total valid response to all three surveys" (Table 4.2) ranged from 40 in San Bernardino County

TABLE 4.2 Response Rate for 1993 Survey

	Contra Costa	Santa Clara	Los Angeles	San Bernardino
Mailed out: 1989 list	609	664	484	499
Mailed out: 1993 only	180	151	158	177
Total valid response (combined)	344	443	258	284
Total valid response to all three surveys	57	62	44	40
Response rate (percent) for 93 combined list	59.6	67.8	54.1	55.6

to 62 in Santa Clara County. As a result, the analysis on individual longitudinal changes in perception and behavior was not tabulated on an county-by-county basis, but instead the responses from the four counties were combined into a single analysis.

Test for Response Bias

Since many of those who responded in 1989 or 1990 either did not return their questionnaires or were different individuals from those we contacted in 1993 (e.g., new residents at the same house), we wanted to ensure that it was appropriate to compare the 1989, 1990 and 1993 cross-sectional responses to determine the existence of shifts in attitude and behavior. We therefore compared the three samples on selected variables--family income, age of head of household and home value--using an analysis of variance. We found that the characteristics of the three cross-sectional samples (1989, 1990 and 1993) were essentially the same, with two exceptions: (1) reported home value was higher in Contra Costa County for respondents in 1993 as opposed to 1989 and (2) income was higher in Santa Clara County for 1993 as opposed to 1989 respondents. The first exception is of little import, since we were sampling the residents of the very same houses in the three years; the shift reflects, simply, a change in overall house values in these areas over the four-year study period. Technically, what we found is that the null hypothesis--that the means of the three samples were the same with respect to age, income and home value--could not be rejected at the .05 level of significance in an analysis of variance. We may therefore assume that the 1989, 1990 and 1993 cross-sectional samples are drawn from the same population with respect to these three indicators.

Advisory Committee

The questionnaire was developed with the advice of a committee of experts. The advisory committee was convened not only to help with the study design, but also to ensure the connection between the research and the needs of the policy-makers, and to facilitate rapid dissemination of the survey findings to key individuals. Members of the committee were chosen so that the research could be based at least partly on the needs of a user community, including the insurance industry, and federal and state regulators. Individuals involved in the assessment and guidance of these projects included several experts in natural hazards, survey methodology and insurance issues, and several key policy-makers representing both state and federal government as well as the insurance industry.

Summary

A sample of homeowners from four California counties were surveyed in 1989, 1990 and 1993. The purpose of the surveys was to document changes in attitudes toward earthquake vulnerability and the adoption of mitigation measures, including insurance. The sample population was divided into two portions: those who responded in any survey in any of the three years and those individuals who responded to all three surveys. The first group was relatively large, in all cases accounting for more than 50 percent and as much as 74 percent of the sample drawn for study. The responses of this group were analyzed to document cross-sectional variability in adoption of non-insurance mitigation measures, earthquake insurance trends by county, and co-variates of insurance adoption, and county-levels of perceived risk (Chapters 5-8). The second population was relatively small--203 individuals in all. Their responses from were combined to investigate trends and changes in individual perceived risk and response (Chapter 9).

5

Adoption of Non-Insurance Mitigation Measures

Is devastation following a major earthquake inevitable? Are there measures individuals, households or governmental units can take to avoid some of the damage and destruction of a major earthquake? The answer to these questions clearly is "yes." By preparing the community, the home and the family before the earthquake occurs, some deaths, injuries and disruption can be prevented, and some of the serious financial impacts of the earthquake can be diminished.

The individual and the household can take part in a variety of activities that can mitigate against some of the serious impacts of earthquake damage. Lists of such activities have been published and distributed by agencies such as the American Red Cross, the US Department of Housing and Urban Development, the Federal Disaster Assistance Administration, and various state and county offices of emergency services. These measures range in levels of commitment and expense--from simply keeping a first aid kit or battery-operated radio ready to investing in structural modifications in the house itself. The purchase of earthquake insurance--a very important type of financial mitigation--will be considered separately in Chapter 6.

Structural Mitigation

Mitigation measures can be divided into two types: structural modifications and nonstructural mitigation measures. Structural measures include anchoring the foundation, bracing cripple walls, strengthening foundations, bracing tall walls or posts (for homes built on hillsides), bracing the garage if there are rooms above the garage, and bracing or replacing the chimney. The cost of these projects varies from as little as several hundred dollars (for anchoring the foundation, bracing the garage door opening or bracing cripple walls) to as much as $50,000 for bracing the foundation. Most of these projects are cost-effective since an unbraced garage door opening, or unanchored or unstrengthened foundations or walls can result in total failure of the structure in a major earthquake (California Seismic Safety Commission, 1992:17).

Since 1991, the need for structural mitigation measures associated with particular houses has been disclosed as a part of real estate transfers. California real estate disclosure laws require sellers of real estate to disclose known defects and deficiencies in the property to prospective purchasers: these defects include earthquake weaknesses and hazards (Civil Code, Section 1102, et seq.). Further, since 1991, sellers of houses built before 1960 must deliver a copy of a booklet developed by the California Seismic Safety Commission entitled, "The Homeowner's Guide to Earthquake Safety," and disclose structure deficiencies (Government Code, Title 21, Division 1, Chapter 1.38). The seller's real estate agent must provide this booklet to the seller so that the seller can provide it to the buyer.

The Hazards Report required for homes built before 1960 includes questions about whether: (1) the water heater is braced, strapped or anchored to resist falling during an earthquake, (2) the house is anchored or bolted to the foundation, (3) exterior cripple walls are braced, (4) any unconnected concrete piers and posts in the exterior foundation have been strengthened, and (5) unreinforced masonry in the exterior foundation or exterior walls has been strengthened. Further, if the house is built on a hillside, questions are posed as to whether the exterior tall foundation walls have been braced, and the tall posts or columns have been built or strengthened to resist earthquakes. If the house has a living area over a garage, the wall around the garage door opening should be built to resist earthquakes or strengthened.

Nonstructural Mitigation

Numerous nonstructural measures prepare the household for earthquakes. The Seismic Safety Commission booklet instructs households on gathering emergency supplies, planning for family reunions, shutting off utilities and so forth, and makes suggestions about what to do during and immediately after an earthquake. Other nonstructural measures include bracing the water heater, purchasing earthquake insurance, setting up emergency procedures at the residence, deciding on an out-of-state friend or relative to serve as a contact point for family members, reviewing safe or dangerous rooms or areas of the house, replacing of cupboard latches to ensure that cupboard doors do not swing open, securing heavy furniture and heavy picture frames and mirrors, storing flammable and hazardous liquids on lower shelves away from the furnace and hot water heater, having on hand a working battery radio and flashlight, rearranging the contents of cupboards, and contacting neighbors to set up neighborhood responsibility plans.

Survey research undertaken about 15 years ago showed that a large percentage of people in the Los Angeles regions were unprepared for an earthquake (Turner et al. 1979). For example, over 40 percent of the respondents agreed with the statement that "there is nothing I can do about earthquakes, so I don't try to prepare for that kind of emergency." To assess whether residents were prepared as households or individuals for an earthquake and its immediate consequences, Turner and his colleagues asked homeowners to answer the following: "Please tell me if you have done any of these [suggestions of various agencies and groups concerned with earthquake preparedness] either because of a future earthquake or for some other reasons, whether you plan to do any of these things because of a future earthquake or for some other reasons, or whether you don't plan to do any of these." Some activities were applicable for all households: having on hand a working flashlight, a working battery radio, a first aid kit, stored food, and stored water; rearranging cupboard contents; replacing cupboard latches; contacting neighbors for information; setting up neighborhood responsibility plans, or attending neighborhood meetings. Other activities applied to families with young children: instructing children about what to do in an earthquake and making family plans for emergency procedures at the residence and for a reunion after the earthquake. Finally, other items applied to owner-occupiers: had they inquired about earthquake insurance, bought earthquake insurance, or structurally reinforced their homes?

Analysis of responses to these questions led the authors to conclude that "most households are unprepared for an earthquake and that the prospect of an earthquake has stimulated relatively little preparatory action" (Turner et al. 1979:101). Although more than 70 percent had a working flashlight, and more than 50 percent had a working battery radio and first aid kit, less than 30 percent stored food and less than 20 percent stored water or took any other precautions. Although 23 percent had inquired about earthquake insurance, less than 13 percent had bought it. Only about 11 percent had structurally reinforced homes. About half of the families with young children had told them what to do in an earthquake, but less than 35 percent had set up emergency procedures in the residence, and less than 25 percent had plans for family reunion after an earthquake.

In 1979, Palm undertook a smaller survey of residents of Special Studies Zones (surface fault rupture zones) in Berkeley and Contra Costa County to ascertain whether residents of these zones who both received and recalled a disclosure that their property is within a Special Studies Zone would be more likely to adopt the same set of mitigation measures as the general population of Los Angeles (Palm, 1981). The study population was made up of recent home buyers who had purchased property within the preceeding six months. The sub-population who remembered and understood the disclosure were more likely to have inquired about earthquake insurance (41 percent), bought earthquake insurance (24 percent), and invested in structural reinforcements for their homes (9 percent). However, they were generally less likely than the Los Angeles respondents surveyed by Turner et al. (1979) to adopt such mitigation measures as instructing children about what to do in an earthquake, establishing emergency procedures at the residence, making plans for reunion after an earthquake, having a working battery radio, rearranging cupboard contents, contacting neighbors for information, or storing either food or water. Thus, studies completed in the late-1970s in both northern and southern California showed a general lack of individual or household preparedness.

Have disclosure legislation and changing conditions in the 1990's resulted in different responses to the adoption of mitigation measures? This is a question that the current study sought to answer.

Survey Findings for 1993

In three of the four counties, more than 75 percent of the respondents indicated that they had adopted at least one noninsurance mitigation measure (Table 5.1). In most cases, this measure was one of the following: knowledge of how to shut off gas, water and other utilities, possession of tools to turn off these utilities, or storage of emergency supplies such as food, water, or first aid equipment. Contra Costa County residents differed from those in the three other study counties in their lack of respondent preparedness: although more than half indicated that they knew how to shut off gas and other utilities, for no other preparedness measure did more

TABLE 5.1 Mitigation Measures Adopted - 1993

	Contra Costa	Santa Clara	Los Angeles	San Bernardino
Any non-insurance mitigation	63.7	77.2	77.0	76.5
Structural Measures				
Bolted house to foundation	21.9	26.0	13.3	9.6
Strengthened garage door opening	10.5	10.7	11.3	10.7
Strengthened exterior walls	5.8	6.8	9.4	2.5
Strengthened cripple walls	5.3	7.1	9.0	4.3
Non-structural measures				
Know how to shut off gas, etc.	56.1	69.4	71.9	73.0
Have emergency supplies	46.8	60.0	66.4	68.3
Stored food and water	42.7	54.3	64.5	65.6
Secured water heater	40.9	55.9	44.5	46.6
Have tools for turning off utilities	43.6	57.5	63.3	61.6
Plans for family reunion after quake	21.6	27.0	31.6	31.0
Secured heavy things in home	18.7	37.0	28.5	25.6
Conducted practice drills in home	6.1	5.3	10.9	9.8

than 50 percent of the respondents indicate that they had taken measures to prepare their homes or their families for a major earthquake.

Respondents were more likely to adopt nonstructural measures than structural ones. In Santa Clara, Los Angeles and San Bernardino counties, the majority had stored emergency supplies, food and water, and had the tools and knowledge to shut off utilities. Only in Santa Clara County had a majority of the respondents taken the simple and effective step of securing their water heater so that it would not tip over in an earthquake and possibly cause a fire. In all four counties, only a small minority had made plans to reunite the family after an earthquake, secured heavy items such as pictures or bookshelves to prevent injury during an earthquake, or conducted practice drills in the home--a cost-free and easy step taken by less than 10 percent of the respondents.

Structural measures were even less likely to be adopted. In Contra Costa and Santa Clara counties, approximately one-fifth to one-fourth of the respondents had bolted their houses to the foundation; only about 10 percent of the respondents in the southern counties had taken this important and relatively inexpensive measure. More complex measures--securing and strengthening exterior and cripple walls or living spaces above garage door openings--were undertaken by less than 10 percent of the respondents.

Factors Associated with Mitigation

Several variables might be expected to be associated with the adoption of various mitigation measures. First, since the hazard disclosure law requires sellers to disclose structural weaknesses of all homes built before 1960, one might expect to observe more structural modifications in housing built in 1959 or before. Second, it is likely that only those homeowners who (1) believed their own home to be subject to earthquake damage, (2) could afford the structural modification, and (3) were aware of effective possible modifications would adopt relatively expensive mitigation measures. Thus perceived vulnerability, income, and, possibly, education might be expected to combine to predict the adoption of mitigation measures. Third, families with small children would be expected to be more likely to make plans for family reunions or conduct practice drills. Other empirical regularities might also be expected. Given these hypotheses, what are the systematic variations in the adoption of non-insurance mitigation?

Age of Construction. In each of the four study counties, responses to the structural mitigation questions were divided between houses built in 1959 or before and those built after 1960. Chi square statistics were calculated for each of these cross-tabulations. It was expected that, because of the disclosure legislation, a greater proportion of houses built before 1959 would have some structural modifications to make them safer against earthquake hazards. With the exception of one mitigation measure in one county, we found no difference between residents of pre-1960 and post-1960 housing with respect to the likelihood that the house had structural modifications to protect it against earthquake-related damage. Only in San Bernardino County were residents of post-1960 houses more likely to have braced, strapped and anchored the water heater, a counter-intuitive finding. In no other county and for no other structural mitigation measure was there any statistically significant difference based on age of housing.

Predictors of Mitigation. We expected that adoption of structural measures would be related to economic variables as well as perceived risk. However, we found no consistent pattern across counties as to individual variables or combinations of variables that were correlated with the adoption of structural mitigation (Table 5.2). Bolting the house to the foundation was related to ethnicity in Contra Costa and Santa Clara counties (Anglos, African-Americans, Asians and Hispanics differed in the percentages who adopted this mitigation measure), but even for this difference the numbers were small and not consistent across the two counties. Income was related to the adoption of structural measures only in Los Angeles County, where people with higher incomes were more likely to have bolted the house to the foundation. Perceived risk and experience with an earthquake were associated with bolting the house to the foundation and strengthening exterior walls and cripple walls in San Bernardino County and strengthening exterior walls in Santa Clara County.

Nonstructural measures were also not consistently related to demographic, economic, risk perception or risk experience across the counties. Perceived risk was the most consistent predictor of the adoption of nonstructural mitigation measures, correlated with conducting practice drills in Contra Costa County, storage of emergency supplies in Santa Clara and San Bernardino counties, knowing how to shut off utilities in San Bernardino County, storage of food and water in Santa Clara and San Bernardino counties, having tools for turning off utilities in Santa Clara and San Bernardino counties, making plans for family reunions in Los Angeles County, and securing heavy objects in the home in San Bernardino County. Experience with an earthquake was also associated with adoption of several nonstructural mitigation

TABLE 5.2 Correlates of Mitigation Measures Adopted - 1993
(statistically significant variables in best logistic regression model)

	Contra Costa	Santa Clara	Los Angeles	San Bernardino
Structural Measures				
Bolted house to foundation experience	ethnicity	ethnicity	income	indirect
Strengthened garage door opening	none	length of time in California	none	equity perceived risk direct experience
Strengthened exterior walls	distance from fault young children in household	perceived risk	none	direct experience perceived risk gender young children in household equity
Strengthened cripple walls	distance from fault	none	length of time in California	direct experience
Non-structural Measures				
Know how to shut off gas, etc.	none	ethnicity	none	perceived risk young children in household
Have emergency supplies	none	perceived risk length of time in California	indirect experience	perceived risk length of time in California ethnicity

Non-structural Measures *(Continued)*	Contra Costa	Santa Clara	Los Angeles	San Bernardino
Stored food and water	direct experience young children in household	perceived risk ethnicity length of time in California	none	direct experience perceived risk length of time in California
Secured water heater experience	none	ethnicity	indirect experience income length of time in California	indirect
Have tools for turning off utilities	direct experience gender	perceived risk ethnicity	indirect experience ethnicity	perceived risk young children in household equity
Plans for family reunion after quake	none	young children in household equity	equity perceived risk	none
Secured heavy things in home	none	ethnicity income	direct equity distance from fault equity	perceived risk
Conducted practice drills in home	perceived risk young children in household	none	none	none

measures: with having emergency supplies in Los Angeles County, storing food and water in Contra Costa and San Bernardino counties, securing water heaters in Los Angeles and San Bernardino counties, having tools for turning off utilities in Contra Costa and Los Angeles counties, and securing heavy objects in the home in Los Angeles County. Income, ethnicity, presence of young children, length of residence in California, distance from a fault trace and gender were only sporadically related to various nonstructural mitigation measures.

Adoption of Earthquake Insurance. In addition to the model predictor variables, we found that the adoption of one form of mitigation--earthquake insurance--was related sporadically to the adoption of other forms of mitigation measures. Those who had insurance in Contra Costa, Santa Clara, and Los Angeles counties were also more likely to have adopted some other type of mitigation measure. There was no relationship between insurance status and the adoption of other mitigation measures in San Bernardino County. When the non-insurance mitigation measures were categorized into structural or non-structural, the relationship with insurance status weakens, with the exception that insured in Contra Costa and Santa Clara counties were also more likely to undertake structural mitigation measures. When the propensity of the insured or the uninsured to take individual mitigation measures was analyzed, there was no consistent pattern across all four of the counties. The most consistent relationships were for the storage of emergency supplies and the knowledge of how to turn off the utilities, more frequently listed by the insured in Contra Costa, Santa Clara, and Los Angeles counties.

Trends in Mitigation

Comparing responses to the survey by Turner et al. in 1977 with those from this survey, we find that the residents of Los Angeles have improved their levels of preparedness somewhat over this 15 year period. We should note that the Turner et al. survey is not exactly comparable to the current survey: the Turner survey used a random sample of the Los Angeles population, while the current survey was limited to owner-occupiers, a selected portion of the population. Despite these very serious differences in the underlying population surveyed, it might be instructive to compare a few of the results from the two surveys. In 1977, 26.8 percent of the households indicated that they had stored food and water; in 1993, 64.5 percent said they took this measure. In 1977, 22.1 percent said they had made plans for family reunions after the earthquake; in 1993 this number was 31.6

percent. In 1977, 50.1 percent had emergency supplies; in 1993 this percentage was 66.4 percent. Finally, in 1977 only 16.3 percent had rearranged their cupboards and secured heavy items within their homes; by 1993 this number was 28.5 percent. We must interpret these apparent changes in the adoption of mitigation strategies with caution, given the different nature of the two surveys. However, there would seem to be increases in the percentage of Los Angeles residents who have prepared their homes and families for an earthquake.

Despite these apparent trends, and despite attempts for many years to increase household preparedness, a large number of residents remain unprepared to survive the first 72 hours after an earthquake: one-third have not stored food, water and emergency supplies, and most have not secured their water heaters, planned for family reunions or conducted practice drills. Even after massive disclosure campaigns, many California residents have not taken even the most basic and inexpensive measures to protect their homes and their families.

Conclusion

The majority of respondents to the 1993 survey indicated that they have adopted at least one non-insurance mitigation measure, usually knowing how to turn off the utilities or storing emergency supplies. In the three counties with the highest levels of seismic risk, Santa Clara, Los Angeles and San Bernardino, most of the respondents stored emergency supplies of food and water, knew how to turn off their utilities, and secured their water heater. Only a small minority of respondents in any of the counties, however, have taken other important and inexpensive measures such as planning for reuniting the family after an earthquake, securing heavy items or conducting practice drills.

Even fewer respondents have adopted structural mitigation measures. In Los Angeles and San Bernardino counties, only 10 percent of the respondents have taken the simple step of ensuring that their houses are bolted to the foundation. More complex and expensive measures to strengthen walls or door openings were almost never undertaken.

Compared with the survey responses from the early 1970s, Los Angeles residents seem to have taken more preparedness measures. However, many are not prepared to survive the first 72 hours after an earthquake. Despite extensive disclosure and information campaigns, many Californians have not adopted the most basic mitigation and preparedness measures to protect themselves and their families.

6

Adoption of Earthquake Insurance

In Chapter 5, we showed that the percentage of Los Angeles residents adopting mitigation measures seems to have increased since the early 1970s. What about the percentage of those adopting earthquake insurance? Several occurrences would be expected to stimulate the purchase of insurance. In this chapter we will review these conditions, report on the survey findings concerning earthquake insurance purchase, and discuss the reasons given by the respondents for purchasing or not purchasing earthquake insurance.

Factors Affecting Insurance Purchase

At the time of the first systematic survey of earthquake insurance subscription (Kunreuther et al. 1978), only five percent of homeowners were insured against earthquake damage. Over the 20 year period since that survey, several events have occurred that could potentially impact insurance adoption: (1) legislation requiring the disclosure of information on earthquake risk and on the availability of earthquake insurance, (2) the occurrence of several moderate-scale earthquakes, and (3) legislation creating mandatory earthquake insurance for the deductible.

Disclosure Legislation

A series of legislation was passed to increase awareness of the earthquake hazard and earthquake insurance as a potential mitigation measure. The two most relevant legislative acts were (1) the Alquist-Priolo Special Studies Zones Act and (2) the earthquake insurance disclosure legislation.

Special Studies Zone Disclosure. The Alquist-Priolo Special Studies Zone Act was passed in March 1972 following the San Fernando earthquake of February 1971. The act was intended to prevent new large-scale development or siting of facilities such as hospitals and schools in areas particularly susceptible to fault rupture. In 1975, the act was amended to require disclosure that a property was in a special studies zone: "A person who is acting as an agent for a seller of real property which is located within a delineated special studies zone, or the seller if he is acting without an agent, shall disclose to any prospective purchaser the fact that the property is located within a delineated special studies zone" (California Public Resources Code, Sec 2621.9). The act resulted in a mechanism by which purchasers of property within one-fourth mile of an active surface fault trace would be informed about the hazard from fault rupture.

This law was amended in 1990 to extend the nature of the hazard zones and mandate disclosure of these new zones. The new law required the State Mining and Geology Board to develop guidelines for the preparation of maps of seismic hazard zones by January 1, 1992, and requires the seller or the agent of the seller to disclose "to any prospective purchaser the fact that the property is located within a seismic hazard or delineated special studies zone if the maps or information contained in the maps are reasonably available." The new legislation mandates the mapping of seismic hazard zones including areas susceptible to "strong ground shaking, liquefaction, landslides and other ground failure." This new legislation extends the nature of the information that must be disclosed to the property purchaser.

Although information is thus available, it is unclear how this information is used in the purchase process. An early study of the impacts of special studies zones disclosure on home buyer behavior showed that most purchasers did not understand or remember the disclosure (Palm, 1981). The question of whether the modified hazard disclosure, mandated in the 1990 legislation, results in increased awareness of individual risk exposure merits future study.

Because of the required disclosure to prospective property purchasers and buyers in the special studies zone, it might be expected that home purchasers would translate this increased awareness of the earthquake hazard into the adoption of mitigation behavior, including insurance purchase. Thus, the disclosure legislation should result in an increase in earthquake insurance purchase, particularly for residents of this designated zone.

Insurance Disclosure. A second form of disclosure legislation was aimed even more broadly at all homeowners who carry homeowner's insurance. Since virtually all mortgage loans require homeowner's insurance, and most owners without mortgages purchase this common home insurance, the target population includes virtually all home owners.

The legislation requires the insurance company to mention the availability of earthquake insurance. In addition, there is no longer any doubt about the fact that fire insurance policies do not cover earthquake damage: the relevant statute (California Insurance Code, § 2, 1081), went into effect in 1984.

Homeowners are informed annually of the availability and cost of earthquake insurance. They should be aware of the existence of this form of insurance and its cost. Furthermore, the annual disclosure itself might motivate some homeowners to consider purchasing earthquake insurance. This legislation is therefore expected to have had some impact in increasing rates of insurance purchase.

Earthquake Experience

A second factor potentially affecting insurance purchase is the occurrence of several moderate earthquakes in California. The reason for this expectation is that preparation for a future earthquake is often at its peak just after a major earthquake with preparedness motivation decreasing rapidly in the wake of the event.

Between the Kunreuther survey in 1974 and the last of our surveys in 1993, five moderate-scale earthquakes occurred. The first was the 6.7 magnitude earthquake at Coalinga in 1983, causing $31 million in property damage and 205 injuries. This earthquake damaged approximately 1000 housing units, about 40 percent of the total in the city. The 1987 Whittier Narrows earthquake had a lower magnitude (5.9) and resulted in no deaths or serious injuries, but it damaged 5000 buildings and caused losses of approximately $358 million. The Loma Prieta earthquake of 1989 was a magnitude 7.1 earthquake. This earthquake resulted in 62 deaths, 3000 injuries, damage to 18,300 houses, and property damage of approximately $6 billion. Two earthquakes occurred in 1992: the Cape Mendocino earthquake near Petrolia (magnitude 7.0), which damaged numerous historic dwellings, and the Landers earthquake (magnitude 7.5)/ Big Bear earthquake (magnitude 6.5). The latter earthquake sequence was the largest earthquake to occur in California since 1952. It caused 1 death and 25 injuries and resulted in property losses to private and public buildings in excess of $90 million (EERI Special Earthquake Report, August, 1992).

These earthquakes are of interest in this study for several reasons. The publicity about the associated damage in both metropolitan areas and relatively isolated areas raised the awareness of Californians concerning their vulnerability to earthquake damage. Second, both the Loma Prieta and the Landers earthquakes were followed by intensive scientific studies revising the probabilities of earthquake vulnerability in California (Working Group, 1992; McNutt and Sydnor, 1990). Third, the two most severe earthquakes--Landers and Loma Prieta--occurred within the study areas in this survey. The Loma Prieta earthquake caused major damage within Santa Clara County, and the Landers earthquake caused damage to property in San Bernardino County. Thus, both earthquakes provided direct or indirect earthquake experience to the survey respondents and could be expected to motivate the adoption of preparedness measures, including insurance purchase.

Mandatory Insurance

Another factor that could have an impact on insurance purchase is the California Earthquake Recovery Fund program, in effect only for calendar year 1992. This program was a new level by involvement of the state in private insurance purchase decisions. The program called attention to the potential need for earthquake insurance as an addendum to the homeowner's policy for those previously uninsured. We expected that this program--even though it was only temporary--would increase the propensity of homeowners to purchase catastrophic insurance.

Survey Findings on Insurance Subscription

The three surveys in 1989, 1990 and 1993 showed a dramatic increase in earthquake insurance subscription from the 1973-74 baseline, and a gradual increase in all these counties over the four-year study period (Table 6.1). Contra Costa County had the lowest

TABLE 6.1 Adoption of Earthquake Insurance for Full Survey Population

County	1989	1990	1993
Contra Costa	22.4	29.3	36.6
Santa Clara	40.4	50.8	54.0
Los Angeles	39.6	45.8	51.6
San Bernardino	29.2	34.6	42.6

rate of earthquake insurance subscription, starting at 22 percent insured in 1989 and ending with 37 percent insured in 1993. The highest insurance rates were in Santa Clara County, starting at 40.4 percent in 1989, jumping a full 10 percentage points in the year following the Loma Prieta earthquake, and ending at 54 percent insured in 1993. The major increase in San Bernardino County was similarly related to a local earthquake--the Landers/Big Bear earthquake sequence. There, insurance subscription started at a relatively low 29 percent in 1989 but ended with more than 42 percent insured in 1993. Los Angeles County respondents showed a steady increase in insurance subscription, to a slight majority (51.6 percent) insured by 1993. Overall, earthquake insurance subscription has increased. However, a large number of households--a majority in San Bernardino and Contra Costa Counties--remain uninsured.

Reasons for Insurance Adoption

Those who purchased insurance were asked to assess possible factors that affected their purchase decision; similarly, those who did not purchase insurance were asked to assess factors important in the decision not to have earthquake coverage. A comparison of the reasons for purchasing or not purchasing insurance in 1989 with the same reasons for 1993, showed that the ranking of factors that affect the purchase decision remained stable over this time period.

For those who purchased insurance, the most important motivating factors, in order of the extent to which respondents said they were "very important," were: (1) "I worry that an earthquake will destroy my house or cause major damage in the future"; (2) "most of our family wealth is tied up in the equity of our house, which might be lost if an earthquake destroyed or damaged it"; (3) "if a major earthquake occurs, the damage to my house will be greater than the deductible, so insurance is a good buy"; and (4) "if a major earthquake occurs the grants or loans available from the federal or state government will not be sufficient to rebuild my house." The mean score for each of these factors was at least 3.5 (where 5 was "very important" and 1 was "not at all important"). The least important reasons for purchasing insurance were "my neighbors or friends or relatives or colleagues convinced me to have earthquake insurance," " my real estate agent encouraged me to buy it," and "my mortgage lender suggested that I have it." The ranking of these justifications for purchasing insurance remained virtually unchanged between 1989 and 1993 (Table 6.2).

TABLE 6.2 Reasons for Purchasing Insurance

Reasons	Rank in 1993	Rank in 1989
I worry that an earthquake will destroy my house or cause major damage in the future	1	1
Most of our family wealth is tied up in the equity of our house, which might be lost if an earthquake destroyed or damaged it.	2	3
If a major earthquake occurs, the damage to my house will be greater than the deductible, so insurance is a good buy	3	2
If a major earthquake occurs, the grants or loans available from the federal or state government will not be sufficient to rebuild my house.	4	4
I saw maps showing hazard areas, and decided I needed earthquake insurance.	5	6
I watched a television program or read an article on earthquake hazards that convinced me to buy earthquake insurance.	6	5
My neighbors (or friends, relative, colleagues) convinced me to have earthquake insurance.	7	7
My real estate agent encouraged me to buy it.	9	8
My mortgage lender suggested that I have it.	8	9

Insurance purchase was thus motivated by anticipated losses, fear that governmental aid will be unavailable or insufficient, and an estimate of likely damages as opposed to the cost of premiums. The influence of family, friends, real estate agents or mortgage lenders was negligible.

Reasons for not purchasing insurance were also relatively stable between the two survey years (Table 6.3). The four most important reasons for not purchasing insurance were: "the cost of insurance was too high for me," followed by "I don't think that an earthquake will destroy my house or cause major damage in the near future," "If a major earthquake occurs, the damage to my house will be less than the deductible on the insurance, so insurance is not a good buy," and "If a major earthquake occurs, the federal or state government will offer grants or loans that will be sufficient to rebuild my house, making insurance unnecessary." Relatively unimportant in the decision not to purchase insurance was the influence of neighbors, relatives and friends, or real estate agents, mortgage companies, and banks. Again, the estimated cost-benefit analysis and the estimated probabilities of the earthquake affecting the respondents' own homes were the most important factors in the decision not to buy insurance; family, friends, neighbors, lenders, and real estate agents were not particularly influential in this decision.

In addition to the questions asked both in 1989 and 1993, we added several questions to the 1993 questionnaire to probe the impact on insurance purchase both of the California Residential Earthquake Recovery Fund program and confidence in the insurance industry. For

TABLE 6.3 Reasons for Not Purchasing Insurance

Reasons	Rank in 1993	Rank in 1989
The cost of insurance was too high for me	1	1
I don't think that an earthquake will destroy my house or cause major damage in the near future	2	3
If a major earthquake occurs, the damage to my house will be less than the deductible on the insurance, so insurance is not a good buy.	3	5
If a major earthquake occurs, the federal or state government will offer grants or loans that will be sufficient to rebuild my house, making insurance unnecessary	4	2
Not much of our family wealth is tied up in the equity of our house, and so we have little to lose if an earthquake destroyed or damaged it.	5	4
I saw maps showing hazard areas, and decided that I didn't need earthquake insurance.	6	6
I watched a television program or read an article on earthquake hazards that convinced me that I didn't need to buy earthquake insurance.	7	7
My neighbors (or the former owner, or friends, or relatives, or colleagues) convinced me not to buy it.	8	9
My real estate agent discouraged me from buying it.	9	9
My mortgage company or bank discouraged me from buying it.	10	10

those who purchased insurance, we asked about the importance in the purchase decision of the following statements: (1) "The fact that the State of California enacted a program to cover the first $15,000 of earthquake damage called my attention to the need for full insurance coverage," (2) "I am confident that the insurance industry will pay out benefits if there is a major disaster," (3) "I know personally or have read about people who were able to collect fully from their insurance policies after disasters--and this has encouraged me to purchase insurance," and (4) "The repeal of the California Residential Earthquake Recovery Fund called my attention to the fact that we needed homeowner's earthquake insurance coverage." Of these factors, the only one that was ranked as important was confidence that the insurance industry would actually pay out benefits in the event of a major disaster. The enactment of the state program was evaluated as relatively unimportant (a mean score of 2.0 on a scale of 1 [not at all important] to 5 [very important]), and the repeal of the program had an even lower ranking (mean score of 1.7). Thus, the California Residential Recovery Fund did not have a large impact on the purchase decision; instead, relative confidence in the insurance industry was an important motivating factor.

In 1993, we asked those who did not purchase earthquake insurance to evaluate the following reasons motivating their decision (1) "I know personally or have read about people who have not been able to collect fully from their insurance policies after disasters--and this has discouraged me from purchasing earthquake insurance"; (2) "I am not confident that the insurance industry will actually pay out benefits if there is a major disaster"; (3) "Because I paid the surcharge for the extra coverage, the State of California is providing for the first $15,000 in damage"; and (4) "I felt the California Residential Earthquake Recovery Fund is sufficient and we didn't need homeowners' earthquake insurance coverage." Responses were similar to those of the insurance purchasers. The California Earthquake Recovery Fund was not an important reason for not purchasing insurance; instead the most important factor was the lack of confidence that the insurance industry would actually pay out benefits in a major disaster. Personal acquaintance with someone who had not received full benefits from insurance policies after a disaster also affected the decision not to purchase insurance. Belief in the sufficiency of the California Residential Earthquake Recovery Fund was relatively unimportant in the decision not to purchase catastrophic earthquake coverage.

Conclusion

Between 1973 and 1993, earthquake insurance subscription increased dramatically in all study counties. The factors that respondents report as important in their decision to purchase insurance are fear of a major destructive earthquake, confidence in the insurance industry to pay claims, a relative lack of confidence in government post-disaster aid, and the decision that the premium/deductible costs of insurance do not exceed the benefits of being insured. The California Earthquake Recovery Fund itself was not reported as a major factor motivating insurance purchase. For those who eschew insurance, the major factors are cost of insurance, the belief that their homes are not particularly susceptible to damage, and a lack of confidence in the insurance industry to pay out claims.

7

Co-Variates of Earthquake Insurance

In Chapter 6, we showed that since 1989 the percentage of owner-occupiers who have purchased earthquake insurance has increased steadily. Insurance purchasers tend to believe that an earthquake will occur, that this earthquake will damage their homes, that government aid will be insufficient to indemnify their losses, and that the insurance industry is likely to be a reliable source of protection. Those who do not buy insurance feel that it is too costly and do not trust the insurance industry. Although we know why people think that they purchase or do not purchase insurance, we do not know what characteristics differentiate the insured from the uninsured: do the insured tend to be older, wealthier, live in areas more at risk from seismic activity, and so forth? In this chapter, we will explore the correlates of insurance purchase.

Expected Relationships

We might expect four general factors to be associated with insurance purchase: relative level of objective risk at the house site, personal experience with earthquake damage, socioeconomic and demographic characteristics, and levels of perceived risk. We will first explore the expected relationships and then examine the findings concerning actual relationships between these factors and insurance purchase behavior.

Levels of Objective Risk

Insurance operates on the principle that risk is spread relatively evenly throughout the population of insurance holders. Thus, an incident or accident to part of the population will occur randomly: every insurance holder has an equal likelihood of experiencing a loss from the risk insured against. The overall likelihood of an event occurring in a given year can be calculated from historical experience, and appropriate insurance rates are calculated.

When this principle of random distribution of risk in the population is violated--when the insured population is disproportionately selected from those most at risk--the provision of insurance becomes more problematic. This condition arises, for example, when only those at greater risk purchase insurance, a phenomenon known as adverse selection. The insurance industry has argued that this condition prevails in the case of earthquake insurance: those at risk are also those most likely to purchase insurance.

Since this study was limited to residents of four California counties, the data assembled here cannot document on a national scale the veracity or falsehood of the insurance industry's claim. It is probable that for the United States as a whole, the claim is correct: residents of California are far more likely to subscribe to earthquake insurance than those in states with lower earthquake risk such as North Dakota, Iowa, Kansas or Florida. Within California, however, earthquake risk is locally variable in type and intensity. Does insurance subscription vary with this distribution of risk?

Risk Distribution. Detailed maps showing predicted shaking following an earthquake have been created for the major metropolitan areas in California. In San Francisco, for example, areas have been classified as ranging from class A (very violent shaking) to E (weak shaking) associated with an earthquake on the San Andreas fault. As illustrated by the map of San Francisco (Figure 7.1), the distribution of predicted shaking is sometimes less a function of simple distance from the earthquake epicenter: ground conditions can vastly amplify the energy, creating possible serious ground shaking at longer distances from the epicenter. In addition, the design and quality of construction of the structure can affect the distribution of damage.

Primary damage to structures is caused by ground shaking. The distribution of ground shaking is affected by two factors (1) distance from the fault segment that slips during the earthquake and (2) local ground structure. At the same distance from the epicenter of the earthquake, shaking is less severe in bedrock than in sedimentary deposits or filled land. Construction on unstable soils suffers damage even when it is distant from the earthquake epicenter: foundations are likely to fail, with major associated damage to the structure. Furthermore, construction in water-saturated sedimentary soils,

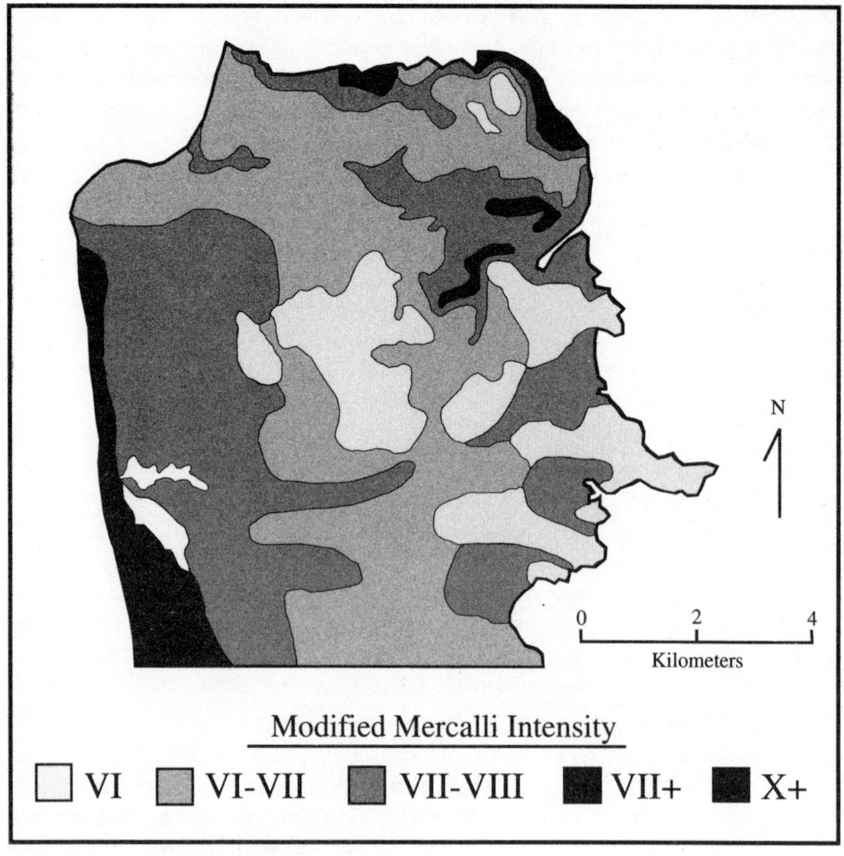

FIGURE 7.1 San Francisco shaking intensities

particularly where land has been created through fill, causes liquefaction of the soil. In liquefaction, the land loses strength and subsides, resulting in fracturing and sliding of the ground surface and failure of building foundations (Figure 7.2). Landslides can also damage buildings on steep slopes. Finally, the surface of the earth may rupture within the fault zones, damaging or destroying buildings in the surface fault rupture zone.

For people to respond to objective levels of earthquake risk, they must be aware that their houses are built in particularly risky areas. What is the nature of public information about seismic risk? Fairly detailed county maps are available that show slope stability (Wieczorek, Wilson and Harp, 1985), earthquake epicenters (Brabb and Olsen, 1986), liquefaction susceptibility (Youd and Perkins, 1987),

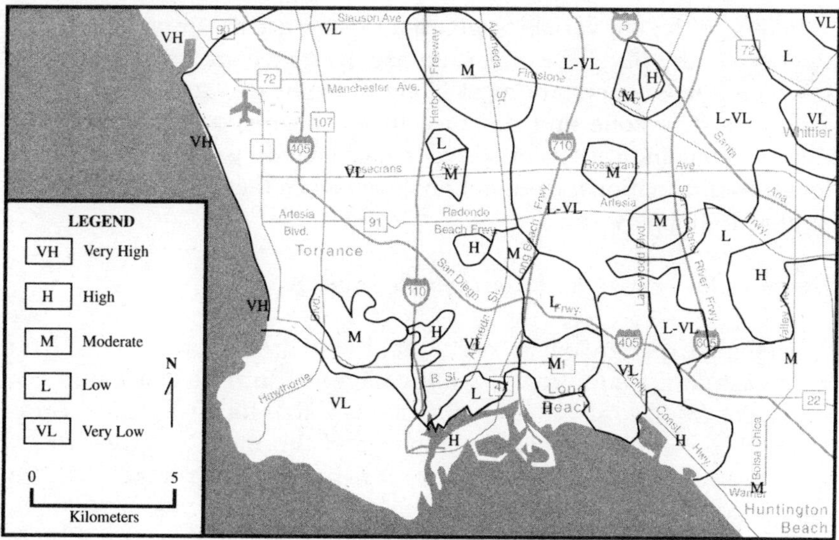

FIGURE 7.2 Areas susceptible to liquefaction

predicted seismic shaking intensities (Thomson and Evernden, 1986), and cumulative potential damage potential from ground shaking (Perkins, 1987). Local newspapers periodically refer to or reproduce these maps, or provide other information about earthquake preparedness. One example is the 1990 distribution of a four-color 24 page supplement prepared by the US Geological Survey and associated agencies entitled, "The Next Big Earthquake in the Bay Area May Come Sooner Than you Think: Are you Prepared?" The impact of such information on individual awareness of relative seismic risk is not well documented (see Blanchard, 1992 for an example of one study). However, it is not likely that most homeowners become aware of the relative likelihood of seismic risk affecting their home because of the availability of USGS studies or newspaper publication of such supplements. The distribution of probable ground shaking, while well documented by scientists, is not widely disseminated in an understandable and memorable form to homeowners.

More direct information on seismic risk comes from the mandated disclosures of special studies zone location that accompany the purchase transaction. All residents of a surface fault rupture zone are required to sign a form indicating that this location has been disclosed to them. Those persons who live closest to a surface fault rupture (within approximately one-eighth mile on either side of a designated fault) have been informed of this location if they have purchased their property since 1976.

In this study, the variables we used to measure the impacts of objective risk on the purchase of earthquake insurance are limited to those of which homeowners are most likely to be aware: location within a special studies zone and distance to the nearest active fault trace. More accurate indications of objective risk, including ground shaking or liquefaction zonations, were not analyzed since they are unlikely to be familiar to homeowners.

Personal Experience with Earthquake Damage

Personal experience with earthquake damage is also likely to have an impact on the adoption of a mitigation measure such as insurance. Experience with an earthquake makes the hazard much more concrete--people have seen their lives and the lives of those around them disrupted by death, injury or property damage. If the earthquake has damaged one's home, the homeowner may be motivated to purchase insurance to reduce the likelihood that he or she will be victimized in the future. The experience of the earthquake grounds the hazard in a real event and demonstrates the fact that everyone is vulnerable to its impacts.

Experience does not need to be direct and personal to have an effect, however. If an earthquake has occurred outside one's neighborhood in another part of the metropolitan area, a barrage of news stories make the losses more human and realistic. Feature stories report the personal experiences of individuals in an earthquake and the responses of federal or state agencies and insurance companies. These vicarious experiences can influence the insurance purchase decision.

Another level of experience can affect earthquake awareness: the experience of a tremor that does not do major damage. The household that experiences a non-damaging but nonetheless frightening earthquake can be reminded of its vulnerability to a more dangerous event. The frightening experience of such an earthquake can thus be a stimulus to purchase insurance.

To document the impacts of experience with an earthquake on the insurance purchase decision, three questions were posed: (1) To your knowledge, has this house or its contents ever suffered damage from an earthquake? (2) Do you personally know anyone whose property (house or its contents) has suffered damage from an earthquake within the last two years? and (3) Have you personally experienced a frightening earthquake sometime within the past two years?

Socioeconomic and Demographic Characteristics

A variety of socioeconomic and demographic characteristics might be expected to predict earthquake insurance purchase. Older families might be expected to purchase insurance at greater rates than younger households because the elderly tend more toward risk aversion and insurance purchase as part of the cumulative adjustments to environmental hazards. Wealthier households might purchase insurance because they are more likely to have sufficient discretionary income to afford the premiums. Those with higher percentages of equity in their house might tend to purchase insurance to protect that equity, particularly if some combination of high equity and high income motivates as well as enables this purchase. Length of time in California might also predict earthquake insurance purchase: those who recently moved to California might be more frightened of earthquakes and therefore purchase insurance, or, in contrast, those who lived in California longer might have more knowledge of the importance of insurance purchase. Gender might also affect insurance purchase; we might expect that women would be more likely to be risk averse and therefore tend to purchase earthquake insurance at greater rates than men. Level of education might also predict insurance purchase: those with higher levels of education would be more aware of insurance as an option. The presence of dependents in the households--individuals over the age of 65 or under the age of 18--might also affect insurance purchase: families with dependents in the household might feel a greater need to protect their financial stability through the purchase of insurance. Even ethnicity might affect the probability of insurance purchase.

To test for the impacts of various socioeconomic and demographic factors on insurance purchase, we asked respondents for the following information: (1) how long have you lived in California? (2) how long has your household lived at this address? (3) what is your age? (4) what is your gender? (5) with what ethnic group do you identify? (6) how many years of school have you completed? (7) how many persons over the age of 65 live in the house? (8) how many children under the age of 18 live in the house? (9) how much do you think your home would sell for if it were for sale? (10) how much do you now owe on your house? and (11) what was your total gross family income before taxes in 1992?

Perceived Risk

The fourth factor that could affect the purchase of earthquake insurance is the extent to which individuals perceive themselves to be vulnerable to earthquake-related damage. This factor more than any other was found to be associated with earthquake insurance purchase in two previous studies of the four California counties by the author (Palm et al. 1990; Palm and Hodgson, 1992).

Within a given culture, at least four factors influence both the extent to which individuals perceive a given hazard as dangerous to them personally and also their willingness to act on this belief. First, individuals vary in the extent to which they give credence to expert advice on the likelihood of an earthquake in a given time and place, as well as advice about the best means for mitigating against such an event. To some, the announcement of elevated earthquake risk is perceived as a serious personal threat; to others, such an announcement is ignored as not particularly important.

Second, individuals vary in the ways they balance costs and benefits. Benefits are not defined or calculated in the same way by all, and sets of alternative actions considered in the analysis vary, costs are difficult to assign in a uniform way. Finally, competing objectives affect individual analysis.

The third factor is the set of beliefs about who should assume the risks and the responsibilities: to what extent does the government have the responsibility to protect households against earthquake damage as opposed to the individual household, for example? Those who believe that they do have and perhaps should have little control or responsibility for their own well-being are likely to attend less to hazard warnings and recommended means of hazard mitigation.

Fourth, individuals vary in the relative importance that they ascribe to the earthquake hazard, as opposed to the myriad of other factors that cause death, injury and property loss. The earthquake hazard must have salience if the individual and the household are to be expected to invest significant resources--time or money--in mitigation efforts. In the absence of such salience, earthquake hazards are simply another aspect of the "noise" bombarding people in modern society.

Although we could not probe the motivations behind variability in perceived vulnerability, we attempted to assess its strength in the study population. We asked four questions to measure the extent to which earthquake hazards were perceived as threatening to the individual (Table 7.1). These questions were also administered to the study population in the 1989 and 1990 surveys.

Correlates of Insurance Purchase

Since the dependent variable, insurance status, can have only two values ("yes" or "no"), the assumptions necessary for the use of ordinary least squares regression analysis were violated. It would be possible to use linear discriminant analysis in such a case, but the assumption of multivariate normality of the independent variables might not be met. For this reason, we chose the logistic regression model for this analysis.

The set of independent variables describing earthquake experience, objective risk, perceived risk and socioeconomic or demographic

TABLE 7.1 Risk Perception Questions

1. Some people have estimated the chances of a strong earthquake (of the size that struck San Francisco in 1906) happening in southern California in the next 10 years as 1 out of 5.

Now, please think about the chances of a San Francisco-type earthquake occurring in your community. What do you think are the chances that such an earthquake would occur in the next ten years in your community?

1 out of ____________________ (number)

2. How likely do you think it is that your own home will be seriously damaged by an earthquake in the next ten years? (circle number).

1. VERY LIKELY
2. SOMEWHAT LIKELY
3. SOMEWHAT UNLIKELY
4. NOT VERY LIKELY

3. What are the chances of a 1906 San Francisco-type earthquake causing more than 10 percent damage to your own home in the next 10 years. One out of how many is your estimate of the chances of such an earthquake occurring in the next ten years?

1 out of ____________________ (number)

4. Suppose a major damaging earthquake occurred in your community--of the magnitude of the 1906 San Francisco earthquake. How much (in dollars) damage would be caused to the contents of your house as well as the house itself?

$________________________________

characteristics was used in combination to classify respondents as insurance purchasers or nonpurchasers. In logistic regression, one estimates the probability of an event occurring (in this case, of an individual purchasing earthquake insurance):

$$\text{Prob (insurance)} = \frac{1}{1+e^{-Z}}$$

where Z is the linear combination

$$Z = B + B_1X_1 + B_2X_2 + \ldots + B_pX_p,$$

and e is the base of the natural logarithms. The parameters of the model are estimated using the maximum-likelihood method--the coefficients that make the observed results most likely are selected.

In the set of logistic regressions reported here, independent variables were entered using a forward stepwise method; that is, they were tested for entry into the model individually based on the significance level of the score statistic. Variables already in the model at each step were also tested for possible removal based on the significance level of the Wald statistic (the square of the ratio of the coefficient to its standard error). The three statistics used to assess the robustness of the classification were (1) the percentage correctly classified by the model; (2) the -2 log likelihood of the model (the closeness of the model to the null hypothesis that the models fits perfectly); and (3) the "goodness of fit" of the model (a comparison of observed probabilities to those predicted by the model).

County Findings

The logistic regressions performed well in distinguishing the insured from the uninsured homeowners (Table 7.2). The combination of variables we hypothesized as related to insurance purchase were effective in distinguishing these two populations. In all cases one could not reject the null hypothesis that the model was a "perfect" one (as reflected by the probability of the -2 log likelihood statistic and the "goodness of fit" statistic). In most cases, the model correctly predicted at least 70 percent of the observations.

In Contra Costa County, the variables in the best model--those that best sorted the insured from the uninsured--were experience with an earthquake (previous damage to the home), perceived risk, length of residence in California, and age. The Santa Clara County model was

TABLE 7.2 Logistic Regressions on Insurance Status - 1993 Respondents

	Contra Costa	Santa Clara	Los Angeles	San Bernardino
Percent correct - uninsured	87.3	63.7	76.1	72.5
Percent correct - insured	49.2	82.1	79.0	58.9
Percent correct - all	74.9	74.4	77.8	66.9
Model: -2 log likelihood	.28	.32	.60	.27
Model: goodness of fit	.50	.83	.78	.81
Variables in the model:	housdm chsf6 doll income CAlng age	chhome doll homvl school	knowqk chhome child	chsf income

Variable definitions:

chhome - How likely own home will be damaged by earthquake in next 10 yrs
chsf - chances of major earthquake in community in next 10 years
chsf6- chances of more than 10% damage to home in next 10 years
doll- percentage dollar damage to home from major earthquake
income- pre-tax family income
homvl - estimated sales price of home
age - age of respondent
child - children under age 18 in household
school - number of years of school completed
CAlng - number of years of residence in California
knowqk - personally know someone with property damage from earthquake
housdm - this house has suffered damage from an earthquake

composed of perceived risk, home value and level of education. Los Angeles insurance status was predicted by experience with an earthquake, perceived risk, and the presence of children under age 18 in the household. In San Bernardino, the model included perceived risk and income level. Overall, the variables that most consistently discriminated between the insured and the uninsured were perceived risk, and income or home value. Those who perceive themselves to be at greater risk are more likely to purchase earthquake insurance. In addition, those with higher levels of income or higher home values are also more likely to purchase insurance.

Variables that consistently do not enter into the logistic regression equations and do not distinguish the insured from the uninsured are levels of objective risk (distance from an active surface fault trace or location within a Special Studies Zone), recent experience with an earthquake (personal acquaintance with a person whose property has been damaged by an earthquake or personal experience with a frightening earthquake within the past two years), as well as certain demographic variables (gender, percentage of equity in the home, presence of persons over age 65 in the household, or ethnicity).

These equations are comparable to those calculated for the 1990 respondents (Table 7.3). The variable that most consistently discriminated the insured from the uninsured respondents in 1993 was perceived risk, although other variables were statistically significant in individual cases (damage from the Loma Prieta earthquake in Contra Costa County, and home value and age of respondent in Los Angeles County).

Insurance status is thus not consistently predicted by the set of expected variables: a combination of objective risk, perceived risk, economic wherewithal and experience with earthquake damage. Instead, perceived risk is clearly the most significant predictor, followed by economic status. Objective risk, experience with smaller earthquakes, and demographic variables are relatively unimportant in distinguishing the insured from the uninsured.

Trends in Co-Variates

These findings generally agree with those of the earlier surveys in 1989 and 1990 reported elsewhere (Palm et al. 1990; Palm and Hodgson, 1992). However, to document the extent to which variable associations have changed between 1989 and 1993, we conducted another set of analyses using only those variables that were gathered in both surveys. Again, the general expected model was that insurance

TABLE 7.3 Logistic Regressions on Insurance Status - 1990 Respondents

	Contra Costa	Santa Clara	Los Angeles	San Bernardino
Percent correct - uninsured	89.9	56.1	73.7	67.8
Percent correct - insured	45.4	80.0	83.8	73.2
Percent correct - all	74.0	69.3	78.7	70.1
Model: -2 log likelihood	.25	.06	.76	.07
Model: goodness of fit	.54	.43	.80	.37
Variables in the model:	Lomadam chsf6 school	chhome doll	homvl chhome age	chhome

Variable definitions:

Lomadam - house damaged in the 1989 Loma Prieta earthquake
chhome - How likely own home will be damaged by earthquake in next 10 yrs
chsf6- chances of more than 10% damage to home in next 10 years
doll- percentage dollar damage to home from major earthquake
homvl - estimated sales price of home
age - age of respondent
school - number of years of school completed

TABLE 7.4 Logistic Regressions on Insurance Status

1989	Contra Costa	Santa Clara	Los Angeles	San Bernardino
Percent correct - uninsured	20.0	65.9	69.6	47.5
Percent correct - insured	93.6	73.3	77.2	87.8
Percent correct - all	74.5	69.9	73.9	75.5
Model: -2 log likelihood	.30	.03	.39	.41
Model: goodness of fit	.63	.31	.60	.59
Variables in the model:	chhome	chhome	housdam	chsf
	chool	doll	chsf6	income
	doll	age	child	doll
	age	school	doll	
	CAlng	chsf6	homval	
		CAlng		

(Continued)

1993	Contra Costa	Santa Clara	Los Angeles	San Bernardino
Percent correct - uninsured	89.6	58.9	80.9	77.4
Percent correct - insured	57.9	81.8	72.6	62.5
Percent correct - all	79.7	72.0	76.2	71.0
Model: -2 log likelihood	.59	.09	.51	.07
Model: goodness of fit	.68	.20	.77	.17
Variables in the model:	chsf chsf6 doll income CAlng age	chhome doll homvl school	child chhome	chsf chhome doll CAlng school child

Variable definitions:

chhome - How likely own home will be damaged by earthquake in next 10 yrs
chsf - chances of major earthquake in community in next 10 years
chsf6- chances of more than 10% damage to home in next 10 years
doll- percentage dollar damage to home from major earthquake
income- pre-tax family income
homvl - estimated sales price of home
age - age of respondent
child - children under age 18 in household
school - number of years of school completed
CAlng - number of years of residence in California
knowqk - personally know someone with property damage from earthquake
housdm - this house has suffered damage from an earthquake

status is a product of some combination of variables that represent objective risk (distance from the fault, location within a Special Studies Zone), subjective risk (all questions listed in Table 7.1), demographic and economic status (school years completed, presence of children under 18 or individuals over 65 in the home, income, home value, percentage of equity in the home, ethnicity, and age of the respondent), and previous earthquake experience (length of residence in California, previous damage to the home).

Equations for the 1989 respondents and the 1993 respondents were calculated (Table 7.4). Although individual variables shifted in the strength of their association with insurance status, the overall pattern remains similar across the counties and throughout the study period. The variables most likely to discriminate the insured from the uninsured are those describing perceived risk. Perceived vulnerability to earthquake damage continues to be the factor that best predicts insurance purchase.

Summary

Logistic regression demonstrates that perceived vulnerability to earthquake damage is a strong and consistent factor distinguishing the insured from the uninsured. This factor has remained strong over the four-year study period, and has been relatively unaffected by variations in earthquake experience, dissemination of information about objective risk or socioeconomic or demographic factors. In Chapter 8, we will explore trends in the primary explanatory variable--perceived vulnerability to earthquake risk.

8

Perceived Risk

Perceived risk, the perceived vulnerability of individuals and households to earthquake hazards, is the most important predictor of earthquake insurance purchase. It is also closely associated with the adoption of non-insurance mitigation measures such as the storage of food and water or structural modifications to the dwelling. But what predicts variability in perceived risk? In this chapter, we will review the overall perceptions of risk within the State of California, the factors that should be associated theoretically with perceived risk, the empirical findings on trends in and co-variates of perceived risk, and the way in which Californians portray the geographic variability of earthquake hazard within the state.

Perceived Vulnerability

Previous research suggests that, within a given environmental and cultural setting, individual variability in perceived vulnerability to hazards is at least in part a function of (1) variability in personality characteristics, (2) proximity to and previous experience with the hazard, and (3) a set of socioeconomic and demographic characteristics.

Personality Characteristics

The first of these factors--the linking of personality characteristics with perceived vulnerability to natural hazards--has been subject to a relatively small volume of intense empirical study by social scientists, perhaps partly because of the difficulties in gathering reliable data. Several studies indicate the importance of the use of personality scales and "fatalism" or "world view" in explaining perceived vulnerability (Simpson-Housley and Bradshaw, 1978; Turner et al.

1979; Drabek, 1986). These studies suggest that individuals who are more generally fatalistic also tend to eschew individual preparedness or mitigation measures. The extent to which such findings can be generalized across cultures (Markus and Kitayama, 1991) or across hazards (Slovic, 1986) has been called into some doubt, however.

Beyond individual variability in fatalism is variability in perceived social consensus about risk and appropriate response. Social behaviors are influenced not only by individual perceptions, attitudes, or feelings, but also by perceptions about the perceptions, attitudes, or feelings of those in the same community or in their peer groups (Asch, 1956; Ajzen and Fishbein, 1977; Cialdini, 1988; Petty and Cacioppo, 1986). Perceived social consensus can influence the individual's evaluation of risk. For example, if an individual believes that many others believe the community is at particular risk, that individual will tend to strengthen his or her perception of vulnerability.

Personality factors can also be seen within a cultural context. An emerging literature in cultural psychology (Berman, 1990; Markus and Kitayama, 1992; Shweder, 1991; Shweder and LeVine, 1984; Stigler, Shweder and Herdt, 1991) suggests the need for a re-examination of the linkage between self definition and other observed behaviors. These theorists suggest that generalizations about decision-making and risk perception based on the notion of personal attributes may be most valid among those who share the attendant assumptions that the self is independent and that social behavior is voluntarily and personally chosen. This theory means that our generalizations may best fit individuals with Western, independent construals of self. In many non-Western cultures, social behaviors may be better understood in terms of socially shared rules or norms or, more generally, the perception of social consensus regarding a variety of relevant issues. We will return to the implications of this idea in the final chapter.

An example of the type of personality-behavior linkage characteristic of Western culture is the concept of unwarranted optimism described in Chapter 1. Weinstein (1989b) suggests that individuals may construct an unduly optimistic scenario about their own personal safety from a given hazard, creating self-serving predictions about future events and the improbability that they themselves will be affected. This seemingly excessive optimism, more characteristic among American than Asian respondents, may result from a particular view of the self as an independent rather than a socially defined entity (Markus and Kitayama, 1991).

Proximity and Previous Experience with the Hazard

Physical proximity to a hazard should induce perceived vulnerability. The operating mechanism here is the linkage between experience or familiarity with the area and knowledge about and response to its hazards. Persons who live in an area that has suffered natural disasters in the past can be expected to be more aware of the risk and the potential for damage. They therefore have higher levels of perceived vulnerability to future events. For earthquake hazards, physical proximity may be expressed in several ways: distance from an active surface fault trace, location within a special studies zone, or extent to which site has been calculated as susceptible to ground shaking.

Previous experience with the hazard in the current or previous residence can also affect perception. In studies of flood hazards, individuals with previous experience were found to have a more accurate perception of them (Kates, 1971; Burton and Kates, 1964; Roder, 1961; Saarinen, 1982), and proximity to the hazards was related with higher levels of concern (Greene, Perry and Lindell, 1981). Weinstein (1989a) suggests that at least three factors may be involved. First, personal experience may affect the perceived likelihood of future victimization, since accessibility from memory influences probability judgments (Kahneman and Tversky, 1979). Negative experiences or bad memories of a previous event will color judgments concerning the probability of recurrence or potential harm. Second, personal experience provides information about the possible severity of the damage or losses associated with the event and makes these possibilities more concrete (Nisbett and Ross, 1980). Those who have actually experienced shortages of food and water, loss of utilities, or damage to their own home will have a far clearer and more intense understanding of the negative impacts that follow even a relatively moderate earthquake. Third, experience reduces uncertainty about the event, lending greater understanding about the effects on an individual's family and the susceptibility of one's own property (Janis, 1967; Averill, 1987; Janoff-Budman, 1985; Perloff, 1983).

Socioeconomic and Demographic Characteristics

Drabek reviews several individual-level social, economic or demographic factors that have been empirically associated with hazard perception. He notes that these factors should not be considered in isolation, but rather each should "occupy a niche within a multivariate model that should be tested across a taxonomy of hazard types" (Drabek, 1986:327).

Among the individual characteristics that have been isolated are: age, gender, ethnicity, and occupation/income. Empirical research has found that the elderly are more aware of the hazard (Turner et al. 1979; Shimada, 1972; Hanson, Vitek and Hanson, 1979), although they also may be more skeptical of the degree to which they are personally vulnerable (Hodge, Sharp and Marts, 1979). Gender differences in perceived risk have been documented: men found to have more accurate risk assessments whereas women have a greater degree of concern about the risks (Leik et al. 1982). Ethnic differences in concern with natural hazards have also been empirically documented (Turner et al. 1981; Hodge, Sharp and Marts, 1979). Income and occupational levels may also affect perceived vulnerability, although empirical research on this topic has not shown consistent patterns (Turner et al. 1979; Kunreuther et al. 1978; White, 1974).

Among the problems in linking individual variables with perceived risk is the absence of a robust theoretical framework that would suggest why ethnicity, gender, age and so on should consistently create one response or another. Nonetheless, individual socioeconomic and demographic factors are frequently analyzed in a search for possible covariations.

Trends in Perceived Risk

In the analysis of the survey respondents, we found a high level of concern about earthquakes. Over the four-year study period, an increasing percentage of respondents in all four counties estimated that there was at least a 1 in 10 chance of a major damaging earthquake affecting their community in the next ten years (Table 8.1). By 1993, this percentage ranged from a low of 56 percent in Contra Costa County (the county with the lowest objective earthquake risk) to a high of almost 78 percent in San Bernardino County and 73 percent in Los Angeles County.

A slightly smaller percentage of respondents estimated such high probabilities of a damaging earthquake causing at least ten percent damage to their own homes (Table 8.2). The ten percent number refers to the amount of the deductible on the standard earthquake insurance policy: if more than ten percent of the value of the home is damaged, the homeowner losses beyond the deductible become indemnified by the insurance company. At least half of the respondents in the two

TABLE 8.1 Estimated Probability of a Damaging Earthquake Affecting Community

Percentage who estimate at least 1 in 10 probability	1989	1990	1993
Contra Costa	48.7	54.3	55.6
Santa Clara	57.8	60.0	63.9
Los Angeles	69.3	71.9	73.4
San Bernardino	64.6	64.0	78.0

TABLE 8.2 Estimated Probability of a Damaging Earthquake Affecting Home

Percentage who estimate at least 1 in 10 probability	1989	1990	1993
Contra Costa	46.6	50.2	50.0
Santa Clara	49.6	56.4	54.5
Los Angeles	61.6	72.2	68.2
San Bernardino	58.0	58.9	72.8

northern counties and more than two-thirds in the two southern counties estimated at least a 1 in 10 chance of such an event affecting their own homes in the next ten years.

Finally, a large fraction of the respondents felt that a major earthquake would damage at least 50 percent of the value of their home. Percentages varied from 38 percent in Contra Costa County to 55 percent in San Bernardino County of respondents who felt that this very large fraction of their home value would be lost in a major damaging earthquake (Table 8.3).

TABLE 8.3 Percentage Who Estimate that at Least 50 Percent of Home Value Would Be Damaged from a Major Earthquake

	1989	1990	1993
Contra Costa	55.1	53.2	44.3
Santa Clara	41.0	34.7	37.9
Los Angeles	33.3	38.3	43.7
San Bernardino	55.6	61.6	55.0

Co-Variates of Perceived Risk

To test for the factors associated with perceived risk, we calculated a series of regression equations using the responses to the four perceived risk questions as dependent variables. Three of the four dependent variables were treated with ordinary least squares regressions, the fourth (with only four possible values for the dependent variable) with ordered logistic regression. The independent or predictor variables used in these equations were indicators of geophysical risk (distance to the nearest fault trace), previous experience with an earthquake (house damaged by a previous earthquake, personally acquainted with someone whose property suffered earthquake damage within the last two years, personally experienced a frightening earthquake within the past two years), as well as socioeconomic characteristics (home value, age, years of school completed, percentage of equity in the house, income level, educational attainment).

In most cases, the linear combination of these variables was a poor predictor of the intensity of perceived risk (Table 8.4). In no case did the percentage of variance explained exceed 38 percent. The variables that were most frequently related significantly to the dependent variable in the best equations were home value (significant in 6 of the 12 regression equations) and some indicator of earthquake experience (significant in 6 of the 12 regression equations and two of the four ordered logistic regression equations). Thus, the variables describing economic status, experience with a previous earthquake, age of respondent, distance from a surface fault trace, length of residence in California and school years completed were generally not closely or consistently related to perceived risk.

Trends in Perceived Risk Co-Variates

Using variables available for the sample populations for both 1989 and 1993, we sought to determine if trends were evident in the strength and nature of the relationships between perceived risk and other variables. The 1989 and 1993 responses to school years completed, ethnicity, age, length of time in California, presence of children under 18 in the household, percentage of equity, distance from a surface fault trace, income, and home value were compared with responses to the three interval scale perceived risk questions analyzed above. The results show a consistent pattern of independence of the perceived risk responses from the set of independent variables describing geophysical

TABLE 8.4 Predictors of Perceived Risk

Dependent Variable: What is the Probability That a Strong Earthquake (such as the 1906 San Francisco earthquake) Will Occur in your Community in the Next Ten Years?

	Contra Costa	Santa Clara	Los Angeles	San Bernardino
Multiple R^2	.19	.24	.29	.32
Variables in equation	homvl	gender howlong income	homvl fright homvl	knowqk ethnic

Dependent Variable: What is the probability that a strong earthquake (such as the 1906 San Francisco earthquake) will cause more than 10 percent damage to your own home in the next ten years?

	Contra Costa	Santa Clara	Los Angeles	San Bernardino
Multiple R^2	.27	.24	.25	.32
Variables in equation	income equity	age dissto housdm	income housdm	knowqk ethnic

Dependent Variable: In strong earthquake (such as the 1906 San Francisco earthquake) how much damage (percentage of home value) would be caused to your house and its contents

	Contra Costa	Santa Clara	Los Angeles	San Bernardino
Multiple R^2	.25	.36	.36	.38
Variables in equation	homvl gender	homvl income gender	homvl housdm	gender school

(Continues)

TABLE 8.4 Predictors of Perceived Risk *(Continued)*

Dependent Variable: How likely do you think it is that your own home will be seriously damaged by an earthquake in the next ten years?

	Contra Costa	Santa Clara	Los Angeles	San Bernardino
Sign of chi square	.00	.00	.01	.01
Variables in equation	howlong school	howlong child dissto	housdm dissto ethnic ethnic	housdm

Variable abbreviations:

homvl = estimated home value
gender = male, female
knowqk = Know anyone whose property was damaged by an earthquake in the past 2 years
howlong = How long have you lived in California?
fright = Have you personally experienced a frightening earthquake in past two years?
ethnic = ethnicity (Anglo, Hispanic, African-American, Asian)
income = household income
age = age of respondent
equity = mortgage debt divided by home value
dissto = distance to the nearest surface fault trace
housdm = Has this house or its contents ever suffered damge from an earthquake?
school = number of years of school completed

risk, previous damage, or demographic and economic status. An example is the equations for estimated probability of a major earthquake damaging their own home (Table 8.5). The equations for the four counties are consistently poor predictors of perceived risk, with only one or two variables significant at the .05 level of probability. The patterns of co-variates are also inconsistent across the counties and from one time period to another, again demonstrating only a weak relationship. We conclude that perceived risk is unrelated to levels of experience with earthquake damage, extent of objective risk at the home site, or socioeconomic or demographic characteristics. Instead, risk perception is an independent dimension, perhaps related to individual characteristics not measured, or to finer indicators of concepts than those measured in this survey instrument.

Table 8.5 Comparison of Multiple Regressions for 1989 with 1993

Dependent Variable: what is the probability that a strong earthquake (such as the 1906 San Francisco earthquake) will cause more than 10 percent damage to your own home in the next ten years?

	Contra Costa	Santa Clara	Los Angeles	San Bernardino
1993				
Multiple R^2	.27	.22	.20	.18
Variables in equation	homevalue	age equity	income housdm	ethnic
1989				
Multiple R^2	.25	.15	.29	.15
Variables in equation	school income	school	income howlong	school

Variable abbreviations: See Table 8.4

Independence of Perceived Risk

To corroborate the lack of association between the economic and demographic variables, geographic risk, and perceived risk, a set of principal component analyses were calculated (Table 8.6). The variables used in the analysis were the three interval scale dependent variables measuring perceived risk, along with income, school years completed, home value, age of the respondent, number of years in California, percentage of home equity, shaking intensity (for the two southern counties), and distance from the nearest surface fault trace. In all four counties, the resulting analysis (varimax rotation on principal components) demonstrates the clear independence of the perceived risk variables from the others, extracting a separate and independent perceived risk factor. The exception to this statement is the variable "doll"--the percentage of home value that would be damaged in a major earthquake. This variable is related to income and home value: those with more expensive homes tend to believe that a smaller fraction of the home value would be damaged in a major earthquake.

The factor structure for all four counties includes a demographic factor (age, length of time in California, home equity), an economic factor (income, school years completed, home value), and a perceived risk factor (probability of an earthquake affecting the community and the home). The variables related to this factor structure fluctuate only slightly among the counties, consistently demonstrating the independence of perceived risk from the other variables.

Geographic Variability in Perceived Risk

Is all of California seen as "earthquake country," or are some areas perceived as relatively more dangerous to live in? Do people exaggerate the risk for places that have recently experienced an earthquake? Do they underestimate risk in their home community? The geographic distribution of perceived risk within California was the subject of this portion of the research.

TABLE 8.6 Principal Components Analysis of Perceived Risk

Rotated Factor Matrices:

	Factor 1 (Demographic)			
	Contra Costa	Santa Clara	LosAngeles	SanBernardino
Variables				
Age	.85	.88	.90	.86
How long in Ca	.77	.76	.79	.80
Equity	.79	.80	.84	.61
Income	-.28	-.23	-.35	-.23
School	-.06	-.27	-.00	.02
Home Value	.22	.31	.04	.23
Percentage of home value that would be damaged in an earthquake	-.13	-.12	-.01	-.02
Probability of major damaging earthquake in community	-.03	-.08	.02	-.00
Probability of major damaging earthquake causing 10 percent damage to home	-.03	-.10	.02	-.02
Distance to nearest fault	.12	.11	-.15	-.03
Shaking intensity class	NA	NA	.23	-.12

(Continues)

TABLE 8.6 Principal Components Analysis of Perceived Risk *(Continued)*

Factor 2 (Economic)				
Variables	Contra Costa	Santa Clara	Los Angeles	San Bernardino
Age	.03	-.00	-.08	-.07
How long in Ca .	.05	-.11	-.15	.11
Equity	.05	.01	.02	.16
Income	.76	.79	.78	.78
School	.69	.67	.80	.72
Home Value	.76	.82	.76	.69
Percentage of home value that would be damaged in an earthquake	-.42	-.41	-.18	-.51
Probability of major damaging earthquake in community	.07	.06	.08	.11
Probability of major damaging earthquake causing 10 % damage to home	.11	.12	.20	.13
Distance to nearest fault	.22	-.15	.06	-.07
Shaking intensity class	NA	NA	.05	-.05

Factor 3 (Perceived Risk)				
Variables	Contra Costa	Santa Clara	Los Angeles	San Bernardino
Age	-.00	-.03	.15	.02
How long in Ca	.01	-.11	-.13	.06
Equity	-.05	.12	.03	-.09
Income	.09	-.07	.04	.02
School	-.03	-.05	.07	.11
Home Value	.17	-.02	.20	.08
% of home value that would be damaged in an earthquake	-.19	-.28	-.21	-.07
Probability of major damaging EQ in community	.94	.90	.94	.94
Probability of major damaging earthquake causing 10 % damage to home	.94	.94	.92	.92
Distance to nearest fault	.05	.07	.30	.20
Shaking intensity	NA	NA	-.01	.12

Not all of California is equally vulnerable to earthquake damage. Furthermore, any individual is familiar with limited portions of the state. The final task in this analysis of variability in perceived risk explores the relationship between familiarity with the region and perceived vulnerability.

Preference for places is frequently measured, and is sometimes popularized in magazines ranking the "best places to retire," the "best places to find a spouse," and so forth. Less preferred places often become stigmatized because of events that have taken place there or because of natural or technological disasters associated with them. For a period after the assassination of President Kennedy, Dallas was associated with national tragedy. Bhopal, Love Canal and Chernobyl still connote technological disasters. The Miami airport may bring to mind the danger of random murders. Or, entire states or regions may be associated with natural hazards: tornadoes in Kansas, earthquakes in California, hurricanes in Texas and Florida.

In addition to the general ranking of places, geographers are interested in the way individuals perceive the safety or risk associated with the home. Informally, we hear that midwesterners believe that tornadoes are relatively safe whereas earthquakes are dangerous; Californians may believe the reverse. At a local level, survey research has found that individuals draw fine distinctions between the benefits of their home territory and the disadvantages of neighboring areas, distinctions that might be lost on outsiders. For example, in a survey of university students, Gould (1966) found that Alabama students viewed Mississippi as distinctly inferior, while midwesterners might have lumped together the two states as equally distasteful; Minnesotans viewed North Dakota negatively, while Alabama students saw the two states as similarly unattractive.

We are interested in the extent to which Californians distinguish among areas within the state with respect to the earthquake hazard, and also in the extent to which they exaggerate the relative safety of their home region. Previous empirical and theoretical work suggests two very different expectations concerning the relationship between location and perceived vulnerability.

The first line of reasoning suggests that people tend to exaggerate the vulnerability of their home area or other areas with which they are familiar. The principle here is that interaction, knowledge and emotional involvement is at its peak in the home location and decreases as a function of distance (Dornic, 1967; Gould and White, 1986). Individuals are more attached to their home areas than to more distant areas and therefore exaggerate both the benefits and the hazards of home (Figure 8.1). An individual's perceived vulnerability would thus reflect a combination of (1) actual, historical evidence of disasters in particular areas (that is, familiarity with local and distant areas) and (2) a tendency to claim that one's own community or region is more vulnerable not because of empirical experience but simply because of greater familiarity. This type of empirical regularity was noted in surveys of perceived earthquake landslide, flood and hurricane hazard in Puerto Rico (Palm and Hodgson, 1993).

A different empirical result is predicted on the basis of notions of "home as haven," and preference for the home region regardless of its empirical characteristics. Sopher (1979:262) describes the word "home" as elastic in scale, referring to house, land, village, city, district or country, and transferring "to those entities the sentiments of warmth, security and intimacy of relationships that are attached to the home as family dwelling." Tuan (1974:99) describes the attachment of people to their home and home territory in ways comparable to the process by which "a person can become deeply attached to old slippers that look rather mouldy to an outsider." Ley (1983:145-6) writes that home is "a word of experience, a word of human relationship . . . a place of few surprises." Porteous (1976:390) writes that "Home is the space-group-time entity in which individuals spend the

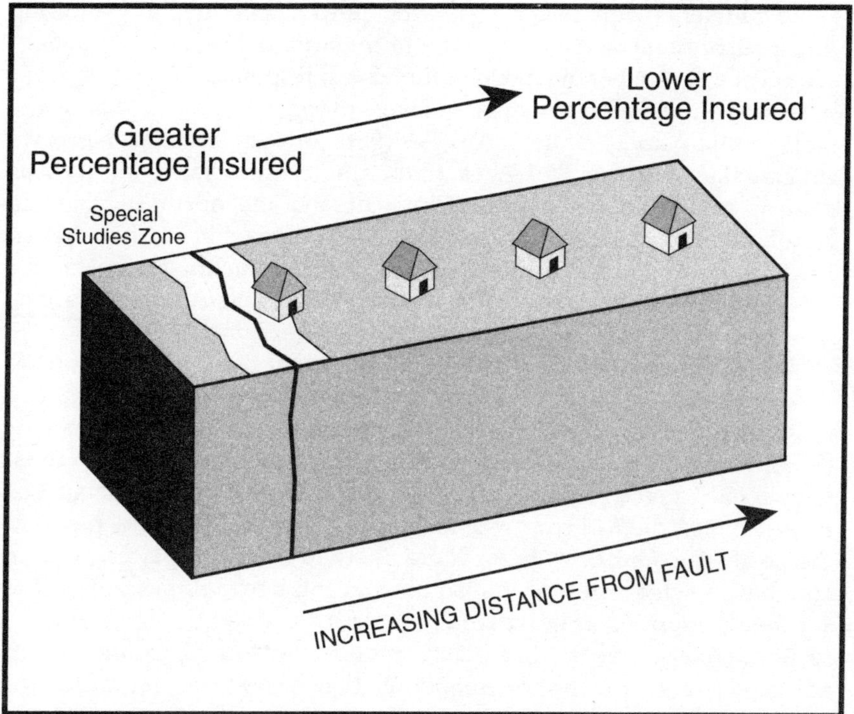

FIGURE 8.1 Distance/Perception Hypothesis

greater part of their lives. . . . Home is a stable refuge for the individual. It provides the territorial satisfactions of security, stimulation, and identity to the most intense degree. "

With respect to natural hazards, home, particularly as extended to the home region, might be expected to be a haven, a particularly safe place. Tuan (1992, personal communication) notes the ironies and ambiguities surrounding the relationship between home and environmental safety: "Generally speaking, home to most people is haven; outside is danger . . . on the other hand, the ultimate secure place (Eden or paradise) is never home but some place far away; and one of the secure things about Eden is that it has no weather--no natural hazard. In other words, home may be haven, but it is also the place where nearly all the disasters of life--human and natural--occur." From this point of view, hazards at home, despite their familiarity, could be underestimated.

Empirical Results

Respondents were asked to list the cities or counties in California "most susceptible to major damage from earthquakes." A respondent could list any number of cities or counties. If respondents selected areas where earthquakes had recently taken place, they would name the metropolitan areas of Los Angeles (site of the Whittier Narrows earthquake) and the Bay Area (including Santa Clara County), as well as smaller areas such as Big Bear and the northern coast in Humboldt and Del Norte counties that had damaging earthquakes in 1992. If they emphasized earthquake hazards in their local areas, their responses showed a regional variability in the number of times they mentioned smaller places.

Respondents followed a pattern of a general notion of earthquake vulnerability in the large urban areas, combined with familiarity with earthquake hazard in the local area (Table 8.7). The major urban areas of San Francisco and Los Angeles were listed by most people (50.1 percent listed San Francisco and 44.7 percent listed Los Angeles) regardless of county of residence. However, respondents from the northern counties were far more likely to list small places in these counties, whereas those in the south concentrated on risks within the southern counties (Figures 8.2, 8.3, 8.4, and 8.5). In addition, respondents tended to list places within their home county or in adjacent counties far more frequently than elsewhere, regardless of recent earthquake history. For example, Contra Costa respondents

TABLE 8.7 Percentage of Respondents Who List Areas as Susceptible to Earthquake Damage

Major Urban Areas:	Contra Costa	Santa Clara	Los Angeles	San Bernardino
Los Angeles city/county	49.7	48.2	51.9	51.9
San Francisco city/county	55.2	51.6	33.7	31.2
More specialized city/county responses				
Alameda	21.2	12.6	1.9	0.1
Contra Costa	16.6	4.1	0.0	0.0
Hayward	9.3	7.0	0.0	0.0
Santa Clara	7.3	25.7	0.0	0.0
Santa Cruz	4.5	20.7	0.1	0.0
San Jose	4.7	11.3	1.2	0.0
Whittier	0.0	0.0	3.9	0.0
Riverside Co	0.0	1.6	14.3	16.5
San Bern'dino	2.0	2.2	24.8	60.0

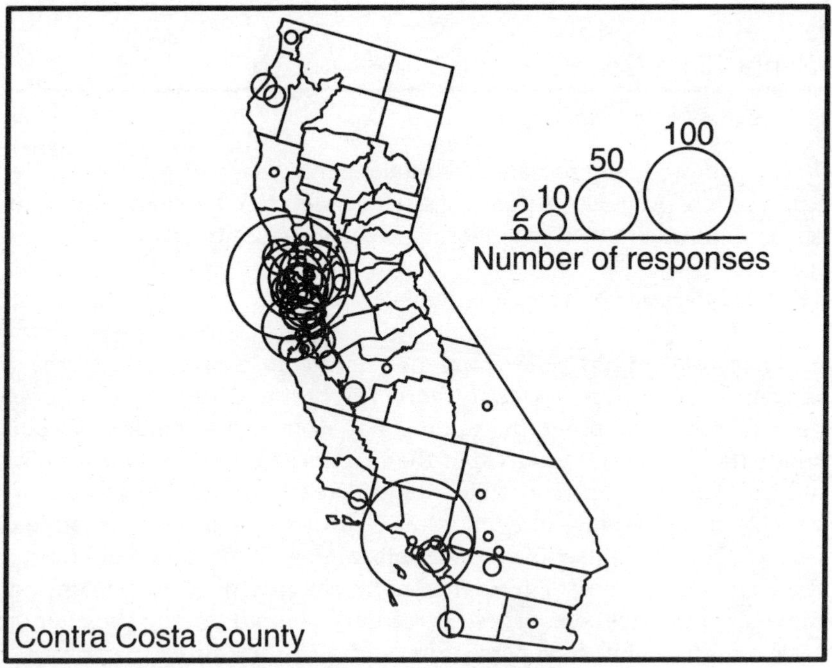

FIGURE 8.2 Contra Costa responses

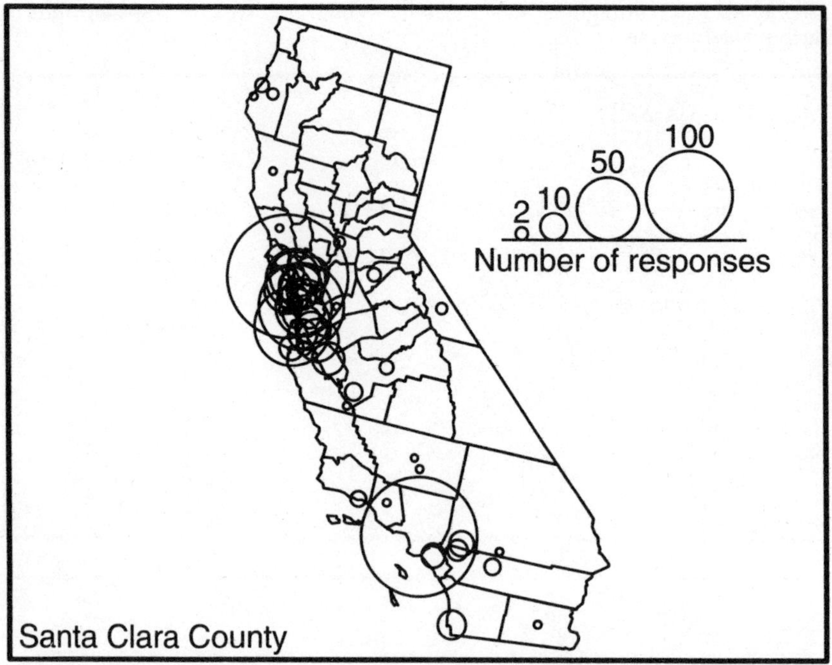

FIGURE 8.3 Santa Clara responses

were far more likely to name Alameda, Santa Clara respondents listed San Jose, Los Angeles respondents named Whittier, and San Bernardino respondents mentioned neighboring Riverside County.

Contrast Between Natives and Non-Natives

Since many Californians are not native to their current area of residence, we believed that there might be differences in areas perceived to be vulnerable among native-born vs. non-native-born residents. We therefore divided the responses into those whose place of birth was the county in which they currently resided and those who were born elsewhere, either within California or in another state or nation. For the full set of respondents, almost 30 percent were born in their current county of residence, whereas just over 70 percent had moved from elsewhere. These percentages varied among the counties from a high of almost 36 percent in Contra Costa County to a low of 25 percent in Los Angeles County (Table 8.8).

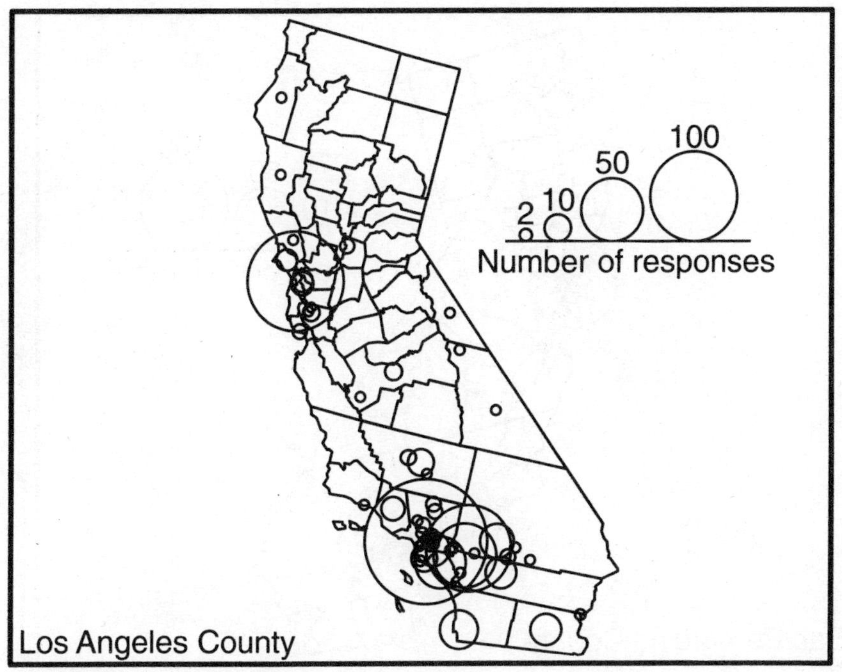

FIGURE 8.4 Los Angeles responses

We then compared the responses of the native vs. non-natives for regional tendency and variability in response. We found that the general patterns remained the same, although the natives mentioned alarger total number of places (Table 8.9).

To summarize, the pattern of areas perceived as more vulnerable to earthquakes is a combination of (1) the home location of the respondent, (2) the location of recent earthquake events, and (3) the major population centers of Los Angles and San Francisco. Recent disasters, particularly those resulting in widespread property destruction, injuries or deaths, tend to become associated with a particular region. In addition, people tend to focus on the earthquake hazard affecting the local area when assessing earthquake vulnerability.

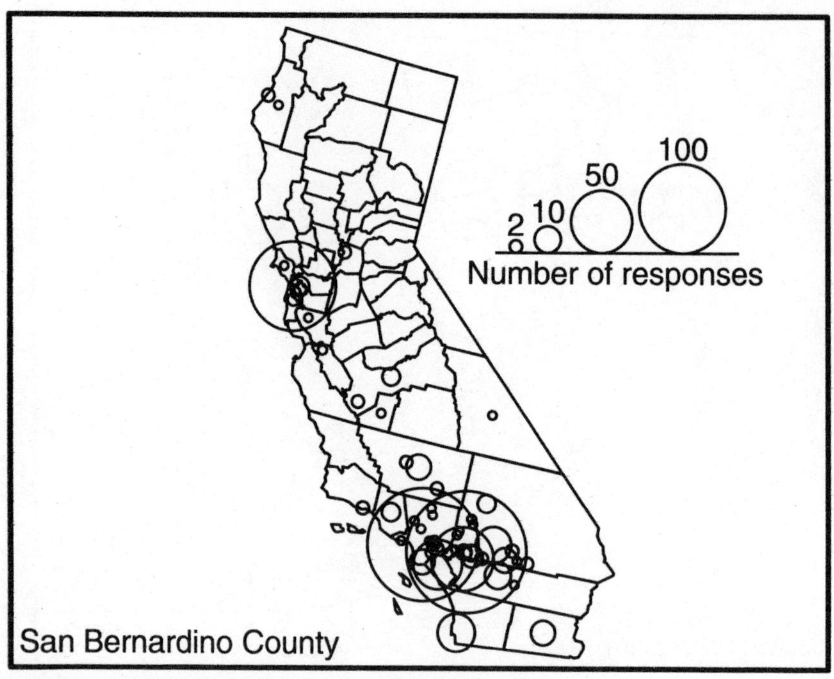

FIGURE 8.5 San Bernardino responses

TABLE 8.8 Percentage Native to the County of Residence

	Percentage of respondents born in the current county of residence
Contra Costa	35.9
Santa Clara	25.8
Los Angeles	25.1
San Bernardino	32.7

TABLE 8.9 Number of Vulnerable Places Named: California Natives vs. Non-Natives

	Contra Costa	Santa Clara	Los Angeles	San Bernardino
Native	38	32	26	35
Non-Native	26	29	19	25

Conclusion

Californians perceive themselves to be highly vulnerable to damage from earthquakes. This perceived vulnerability has increased in each of the counties over the four years of the study period. Socioeconomic and demographic variables, levels of objective risk, or experience with previous earthquakes are not good general predictors of perceived vulnerability.

There is also a clear spatial pattern to areas perceived to be at risk: respondents tend to believe that their home areas are particularly vulnerable to future earthquakes, exaggerating their perceived risk levels above those that would be predicted by past earthquake events.

We have analyzed the results of the three separate surveys but have not considered changes in responses by that small subset of the same individuals who responded to each of the three surveys. In Chapter 9, we will consider the trends in these data.

9

Results of Longitudinal Study

One unique aspect of this series of surveys was the opportunity to monitor changes in both insurance purchase and also attitudes toward earthquake hazards in the same individuals during the four-year study period. This information supplements the conclusions drawn from analysis of the cross-sectional random samples and corroborates the observation that the overall shifts observed throughout the study period actually reflecting changes in attitudes and behaviors in individual households. We were particularly interested in two questions: (1) Are the individual households monitored from 1989 to 1993 changing with respect to their propensity to purchase earthquake insurance? and (2) Are the attitudes of these households with respect to perceived vulnerability to earthquakes undergoing changes? Before considering these two questions, it is important to note the major methodological difficulty encountered in this portion of the research and suggest caution in the interpreting these data as reflecting responses of the general population.

Attrition from Original Random Sample

The population for which we have longitudinal data is far smaller and probably not representative of the full 1989 sample. This lack of representativeness results from the high attrition rate in respondents.

The original survey in 1989 was sent to 864 households in Contra Costa County, 855 in Santa Clara County, 743 in Los Angeles County and 683 in San Bernardino County, or to a total of 3145 California households. The original mailing list contained a large number of errors--addresses that did not exist or individuals who had moved with no forwarding addresses. Of the more than 3000 surveys mailed, only

1786 completed surveys were mailed back (or approximately 57 percent of the total names and addresses drawn), of which 1512 (48 percent of the grand total) had valid responses.

In the second round of surveys (1990), we mailed questionnaires to the same name/address of the household as we had used in the first survey. We did not request that the same individual fill out the questionnaire in 1990 as in 1989. Of the 1512 questionnaires mailed in the 1990 survey, 1071 were returned with valid responses (71 percent).

Thus, the 1993 survey started with a potential of just over 1000 households which had responded in both 1989 and 1990. But it is conceivable that different members of the household responded in these two years. To ensure an analysis of only those individuals who had responded to the survey in all three years, we added two questions in 1993: "Did you personally respond to a similar survey from us in 1989?" and "Did you personally respond to a similar survey from us again in 1990?" Only those who responded "yes" to both questions were included in the following analysis of longitudinal changes in individuals.

Finally, in order to be as accurate and conservative as possible in accepting responses as emanating from the same individuals, we checked this set with respect to demographic variables such as age of respondent and length of residence in California. Responses to those questions in 1993 were cross-checked with answers given in 1989, and cases of variation from expected change (for example, age something other than four years older in 1993 than in 1989) were eliminated.

More individuals than are apparent from the responses probably participated in the earlier surveys; many of those who did not remember responding to "a similar survey from us" in these two previous years probably were survey respondents. There are two parts to this problem: one is recollection of the survey after a period of three years, and the second is a change in the meaning of the term "from us." Because individual households respond to a number of inquiries each year, many people who actually filled out the questionnaire in both 1989 and 1990 probably did not remember three years later than they had responded. Since we did not record names of respondents to the three surveys, we must accept respondents' recollections: that they do not remember the earlier surveys, whether or not they actually were respondents.

The second problem is the meaning of the words "from us." The 1989 and 1990 surveys were administered from the University of Colorado; the 1993 survey came from the University of Oregon. Some respondents may have believed that the third survey came from an entirely different organization, causing them to believe that they did not fill out earlier questionnaires "from us."

In any case, because of survey attrition, the respondents' belief that they had not filled out an earlier survey, change of address of the principal investigator, or other reasons, very small numbers of respondents indicated that they personally filled out both earlier surveys: 43 in Contra Costa County, 44 in Santa Clara County, 33 in Los Angeles County and 29 in San Bernardino County. Thus, for the longitudinal survey population we are considering the set of 149 individuals who claim to have responded to the questionnaire in all three years and whose 1993 demographic characteristics correspond with the 1989 respondent. This population is not representative of the owner-occupiers of the source counties, but nonetheless it is interesting to note the shifts in attitudes and behavior that have occurred in this population of survey "survivors."

Longitudinal Survey Population

The longitudinal survey population is similar to the 1993 full cross-sectional sample. The vast majority (88 percent) are white, with Asians, African-Americans and Hispanics comprising the remaining 12 percent of the respondent population. Most respondents--about two-thirds--are male. In comparison with the general population in California, the respondents are above-average in income, home value and age, reflecting the general tendency for homeowners to be above the population average in these characteristics. The average age of the respondent is 52 years, and the average respondent has lived In California for almost 38 years. The average respondent is in the $50,000-70,000 income category and has completed more than 15 years of school.

To test for any systematic bias in the socioeconomic or demographic characteristics of the longitudinal respondents as opposed to the cross-sectional respondents, we calculated a series of t-tests on length of residence in California, age of respondent, number of school years completed, home value and income class (Table 9.1). In no case could we reject the null hypothesis that the mean of the longitudinal respondents is different from the mean of the general survey respondents: the subsample of longitudinal respondents is thus similar with respect to these characteristics to the full 1993 sample.

Earthquake Insurance Trends

The percentage of longitudinal respondents with earthquake insurance increased steadily throughout the 1989-1993 study period (Table 9.2). The greatest increase occurred in Santa Clara County, the county most affected by the 1989 Loma Prieta earthquake. Here, by the end of the study period, more than 60 percent of the respondents had earthquake insurance. A similar jump in percentage insured occurred in San Bernardino County, the site of the Landers earthquake; at the end of the third survey over 50 percent of the continuing respondents were insured. This increase in percentage insured is also reflected in the observed trends for the cross-sectional respondents (Table 9.2), although the repeat respondents had higher percentages of insurance subscription in all counties except Contra Costa.

The longitudinal survey population was asked their reasons for purchasing or not purchasing earthquake insurance (Table 9.3). Their rankings of factors that were more or less important in the insurance decision are virtually identical to those of the cross-sectional survey population. Furthermore, these factors were stable over the period of

TABLE 9.1 Comparison of Longitudinal and General Survey Respondents Means

Variable	Longitudinal	1993 Cross-Sectional
Length of time in California	37.8	36.1
Age of respondent	52.2	52.0
School years completed	15.1	15.0
Home value	$299,510	$300,386
Income category	4.7	4.6

TABLE 9.2 Trends in Insurance Purchase

Year	Contra Costa	Santa Clara	Los Angeles	San Bernardino	All
1989	18.6	38.6	45.5	31.0	32.9
1990	27.9	51.2	51.5	44.8	43.0
1993	33.3	62.8	57.6	51.7	51.7
Percentage change					
89-90	9.3	12.6	6.0	13.8	11.1
90-93	5.6	11.4	6.1	6.9	8.3
1993- cross-sectional respondents					
	36.6	54.0	51.6	42.4	46.8

TABLE 9.3 Reasons for Purchasing Insurance: Longitudinal Respondents

Reasons	Rank in 1993	Rank in 1989
I worry that an earthquake will destroy my house or cause major damage in the future.	1	1
Most of our family wealth is tied up in the equity of our house, which might be lost if an earthquake destroyed or damaged it.	2	3
If a major earthquake occurs, the damage to my house will be greater than the deductible, so insurance is a good buy.	3	2
If a major earthquake occurs, the grants or loans available from the federal or state government will not be sufficient to rebuild my house.	4	4
I saw maps showing hazard areas, and decided I needed earthquake insurance.	5	6
I watched a television program or read an article on earthquake hazards that convinced me to buy earthquake insurance.	6	5
My neighbors (or friends, relative, colleagues). convinced me to have earthquake insurance.	7	7
My real estate agent encouraged me to buy it.	8	9
My mortgage lender suggested that I have it.	9	8

the study: the top three factors motivating insurance purchase in both surveys are worry that an earthquake would destroy the house, concern about the percentage of family wealth tied up in equity, and assessment of the expected amount of damage to the house in excess of the insurance deductible. Individuals such as neighbors, real estate agents and mortgage lenders were relatively unimportant in influencing the insurance purchase decision.

Correlates of Insurance Purchase Trends

Using the same procedures described for the analysis of the full sample, logistic regressions were calculated for the longitudinal sample. Insurance status in 1993 is the dependent variable, and the independent or predictor variables include previous experience with an earthquake, perceived risk, economic status (home value, income, school years completed), demographic status (gender, presence of children under age 18 in the household, age of respondent), ethnicity, length of residence in California, and distance from an active fault trace (Table 9.4). The resulting equation is statistically significant, and the variables most closely related to insurance status are earthquake experience, perceived risk, and home value. This model is consistent with that for the larger cross-sectional set of 1993 respondents as reported in Chapter 7.

When only those variables collected both in 1989 and 1993 for the longitudinal sample are used in the equations, it is possible to assess shifts in the strength of predictor variables. Two logistic regressions were calculated for the longitudinal sample to compare the predictive value of the same set of variables for the 1989 insured population and the 1993 insured population (Table 9.5). These regression analyses demonstrate the overwhelming importance of perceived risk (chhome) in predicting insurance status in 1989, and the addition of home value

TABLE 9.4 Logistic Regressions on Insurance Status: 1993 Variables

	Longitudinal Respondents
percent correct--uninsured	61.7
percent correct--insured	68.0
percent correct--all	65.0
model: -2 log likelihood	.19
Model: goodness of fit	.58
Variables in the model:	chhome doll homvl knowqk

Variable definitions:
chhome--How likely own home will be damaged by earthquake in next 10 yrs
doll--percentage dollar damage to home from major earthquake
homvl--estimated sales price of home
knowqk--personally know someone with property damage from earthquake

TABLE 9.5 Logistic Regressions on Insurance Status: Only Variables Used in Both 1989 and 1993 Surveys

	Longitudinal Respondents	
	1993	1989
percent correct--uninsured	0.0	75.0
percent correct--insured	100.0	66.0
percent correct--all	64.1	70.4
model: -2 log likelihood	.05	.13
Model: goodness of fit	.37	.58
Variables in the model:	homvl doll	chhome

Variable definitions:
chhome--How likely own home will be damaged by earthquake in next 10 yrs
doll- percentage dollar damage to home from major earthquake
homvl--estimated sales price of home

and perceived dollar damage to the home (variables not independent of one another) in predicting the 1993 insured population.

A third set of logistic regressions were calculated to assess change in insurance status for the longitudinal respondents between 1989 and 1993, with insurance status in 1989 as one of the independent variables. As in the cross-sectional analysis by county reported in Chapter 7, we expected that change in insurance status would be related to a combination of (1) personal experience with earthquake damage, (2) levels of objective geophysical risk, (3) socioeconomic and demographic characteristics, and (4) perceived risk. Experience with earthquake damage is represented by answers to questions such as whether or not respondents' own houses had been damaged by an earthquake, whether they personally knew someone whose property had suffered damage from an earthquake, or whether they had personally experienced a frightening earthquake within the past two years. Objective geophysical risk is indicated by distance from an active surface fault trace. The socioeconomic and demographic characteristics analyzed are ethnicity, presence of children under the age of 18 in the household, number of school years completed, gender of the respondent, length of residence in California, income level, home value, and percentage of equity in the home. Perceived risk is measured by the four risk questions concerning estimates of probabilities of major earthquakes affecting the home and the community (Table 7.1).

Logistic regressions were used to identify the set of variables that best summarized change in insurance status between the initial year of the survey and the final year (Table 9.6) As might be expected, insurance status in 1989 is the best single predictor of insurance status in 1993. The other variables that best predicted change in status are perceived risk and home value. These were the same variables that were most closely related to 1993 insurance status

In addition, regressions were calculated to assess correlates of change in status from insured to uninsured, or from uninsured to insured, between 1989 and 1990, and again between 1990 and 1993. The influences on 1990 to 1993 changes were hypothesized to be the same set of socioeconomic, demographic, distance, and perceived risk variables discussed above.

TABLE 9.6 Logistic Regressions on Change in Insurance Status: 1989-1993

	Longitudinal Respondents
percent correct--uninsured	97.9
percent correct--insured	80.0
percent correct--all	88.7
model: -2 log likelihood	.99
Model: goodness of fit	.96
Variables in the model:	insured doll homvl

Variable definitions:
insured--insurance status in 1989
doll--percentage dollar damage to home from major earthquake
homvl--estimated sales price of home

Among the longitudinal respondents, 15 changed status between 1989 and 1990 (all formerly uninsured who became insured), and 13 households changed insurance status between 1990 and 1993--one who had insurance in 1990 dropped it in 1993, and 12 who did not have it in 1990 had adopted it by 1993. The logistic regression that best classified these changes for both of the years had only a single variable: insurance status in the previous year (Table 9.7 and 9.8).

TABLE 9.7 Logistic Regressions on Change in Insurance Status 1989-90

	Longitudinal Respondents
percent correct--uninsured	78.6
percent correct--insured	100.0
percent correct--all	90.2
model: -2 log likelihood	.99
Model: goodness of fit	.99
Variables in the model:	insured, 1989

TABLE 9.8 Logistic Regressions on Change in Insurance Status 1990-93

	Longitudinal Respondents
percent correct-- uninsured	97.9
percent correct-- insured	87.9
percent correct-- all	92.4
model: -2 log likelihood	1.00
Model: goodness of fit	.43
Variables in the model:	insured, 1990

Trends in Risk Perception

The longitudinal sample population was asked about perceived risk in all three surveys. We found that perceived vulnerability of the home and the community to earthquake damage increased over the study period (Table 9.9). Although in 1989 just over 60 percent estimated that there was at least a 1 in 10 probability of a major, damaging earthquake affecting their community in the next ten years, over 75 percent had this estimate by 1993. Similarly, the percentage who felt that there was at least a 1 in 10 probability that a major earthquake would cause at least ten percent damage to their own home in the next ten years increased from 57 to 64 percent over the study period. The only variable that remained constant was the percentage who felt that such an earthquake would cause at least 50 percent damage to their home value--slightly declining over the study years from 43 to 41 percent.

TABLE 9.9 Changes in Perceived Risk: Longitudinal Population

Percentage who estimate at least 1 in 10 probability

	1989	1990	1993
Estimated probability of a damaging earthquake affecting their community.	63.1	68.6	75.7
Estimated probability of a damaging earthquake affecting their home.	57.0	65.2	64.0
Percentage who estimate that at least 50 percent of their home value would be damaged from a major earthquake.	43.3	42.4	41.4

A set of multiple regressions was calculated on current levels of perceived vulnerability in the longitudinal sample to document factors related to changes in perceived vulnerability. Previous levels of perceived vulnerability were used as one of the independent variables. The hypothesized results were that 1993 levels of perceived vulnerability would be a function of 1989 levels, plus the set of demographic, economic and locational factors used in the previous analyses (Table 9.10).

Contrary to the expected model, however, the empirical analysis shows that indicators of perceived risk are generally unrelated to other variables in the study, with low values for the multiple correlation coefficient. This finding is identical to that for the cross-sectional analysis. The best explanatory variable for 1993 perceived vulnerability is the 1989 measurement for the same variable. This finding indicates a general stability in perceived risk, as well as the independence of this perceived risk from variables in the analysis. Variables that predicted change in perceived risk for the longitudinal sample are economic indicators (home value and equity), and age for pereived vulnerability of the home.

TABLE 9.10 Predictors of Changes in Perceived Risk

Dependent Variable: What is the probability that a strong earthquake (such as the 1906 San Francisco earthquake) will occur in your community in the next ten years? (CHSF)

	89-93	89-90	90-93
Multiple R^2	.12	.11	.11
Variables in equation	chsf89	chsf89 homvl	chsf90 homvl

Dependent Variable: What is the probability that a strong earthquake (such as the 1906 San Francisco earthquake) will cause more than 10 percent damage to your own home in the next ten years?(CHSF06)

Multiple R^2	.26	.20	.32
Variables in equation	chsf0689 homvl age	income chsf0690 how long	chsf0690 homvl income how long

Dependent Variable: In strong earthquake (such as the 1906 San Francisco earthquake) how much damage (percentage of home value) would be caused to your house and its contents? (DOLL)

Multiple R^2	.33	.21	.30
Variables in equation	doll89 equity	doll80	doll90

Summary

For a longitudinal analysis, we followed approximately 150 individuals over a 4-year period, noting trends in indicators of perceived vulnerability to earthquake hazards and in their adoption of earthquake insurance. Based on responses from these individuals, we can corroborate the findings of the cross-sectional analysis that California residents have increased their perceived vulnerability to earthquake hazards and that they have increased their tendency to adopt economic mitigation measures such as earthquake insurance. The factor most closely associated with the adoption of earthquake insurance is perceived vulnerability to earthquake damage--the belief that one's own home will be damaged by a major earthquake within the near future. Recent insurance adoption is also associated with home value and income: those with more resources have a greater propensity to purchase earthquake insurance.

10

Policy Implications

This monograph reports on the results of a study that spans five years and involves three separate surveys of California homeowners. The surveys show a slow but persistent increase in earthquake insurance subscription and a gradual increase in perceived vulnerability to the earthquake hazard. However, the majority of California homeowners remain uninsured and resistant to purchasing catastrophic earthquake insurance as currently marketed. Further, very large percentages continue to eschew even relatively simple and inexpensive mitigation measures that would increase their safety and reduce property damage. These findings have important implications for further state and federal programs.

Perceived Risk

Between the first survey in 1989 and the last in early 1993, one major earthquake and several moderate earthquakes occurred in California. Also, during this period, the United States Geological Survey issued revised predictions for major damaging earthquakes in both northern and southern California. Not surprisingly, respondents reported a slight increase in perceived vulnerability. By 1993, over half of the Contra Costa County respondents and more than three-fourths of the San Bernardino County respondents felt that there was at least a 1 in 10 probability of a major damaging earthquake in their community within the next ten years.

The percentages of respondents who felt such an earthquake would cause at least 50 percent damage to their home value declined in Contra Costa and Santa Clara counties (from 55 to 44 percent and from 41 to 38 percent, respectively) over the study period, but rose in Los Angeles County and remained stable in San Bernardino County. Clearly, very large percentages of the population felt that such an earthquake would cause major damage to their own homes.

Insurance Subscription

An earlier comprehensive survey in 1973-74 of California insurance subscription had noted that only 5 percent of homeowners carried earthquake insurance (Kunreuther et al. 1978). By 1989, our surveys showed that the percentage of homeowners covered by earthquake insurance had greatly increased, ranging from a low of 22 percent in Contra Costa County to a high of 40 percent in Santa Clara County. By 1993 these numbers had increased further, ranging from 37 percent in Contra Costa County to 54 percent in Santa Clara County. Since the four surveyed counties were expected to have relatively higher rates of insurance subscription than the rate for all California, we estimate that the earthquake insurance subscription rate for the state as a whole is well under 50 percent for owner-occupiers. Thus, despite dramatic increases in the adoption of earthquake insurance, a majority of homeowners are still not covered against losses associated with earthquakes.

Those who adopt insurance continue to list similar reasons to justify its purchase: fear that an earthquake will destroy the house and fear that a major earthquake will cause losses greater than the deductible. Those who eschew insurance note that the cost is high and that they do not believe that an earthquake will damage their homes in the near future.

Statistical tests validate the respondents' reasons for buying or not buying insurance: insurance adopters have higher levels of perceived vulnerability to the earthquake hazard and also tend to have more expensive homes than those who do not have earthquake insurance.

Structural and Non-Structural Mitigation Measures

The majority of the survey respondents assert that they have adopted some form of non-insurance mitigation measure. In most cases, this measure is knowing how to shut off the gas or utilities, having emergency supplies, and storing food and water. A small percentage took basic steps to secure their house. Such measures include ensuring that the house is bolted to the foundation or that exterior or cripple walls are strengthened, or securing their hot water heater. Most have not secured heavy items in their home, planned a reunion after the earthquake or conducted practice drills in the home.

Respondents who adopt various mitigation measures tend to be those who have had direct experience with an earthquake, who have higher levels of perceived risk, or who have lived in California for a longer period of time. In addition, those who have earthquake insurance are also more likely to have adopted other mitigation measures. These relationships are not consistent across counties, however.

A great deal of time, effort and money has been invested in information campaigns to increase awareness of the earthquake hazard and associated steps that individuals can take to decrease personal vulnerability. Despite these information campaigns, most of the respondents have not taken even simple and inexpensive measures that would increase the likelihood of survival and reduce injuries and damage.

Implications for State and Federal Programs

Many survey respondents show a persistent resistance to the adoption of voluntary earthquake insurance. Since the pricing structure (the combination of premiums and deductibles) is a major reason given by the uninsured for their decision, it is unlikely that without a major shift in insurance pricing or marketing there will be further dramatic changes in the percentage of households that adopt earthquake insurance. This finding suggests that if a policy goal is universal coverage, major revisions must be made in the way earthquake insurance is offered. One approach might be a federally subsidized insurance scheme, comparable to that for flood insurance. Or, alternatively, the State of California might revise the 1992 California Residential Earthquake Recovery Fund to provide state-backed, mandatory insurance coverage.

Resistence to insurance and to other mitigation programs may also be abetted by public and nongovernmental assistance policies that fail to provide mitigation incentives (White, 1994). Public and nongovernmental assistance policies will need to be coupled with encouragement of basic steps to prevent and reduce losses if we are to see major changes in the adoption of a variety of mitigation measures.

Implications for Future Research

This set of research projects has focused on the response of owner-occupiers in California. The respondents are a relatively homogeneous group of generally Anglo, middle-aged, middle-class residents who own their own homes. Since we are ultimately interested in understanding the general response of impacted populations to environmental hazards, it will be important to supplement this work with studies of a broader selection of people. Not only should future studies investigate contrasts in interpretation of and response to earthquake hazards among a variety of California populations, but further research should employ explicitly cross-cultural research designs to ensure that generalizations drawn from this kind of sample population are not overinterpreted and applied inappropriately to other populations. As we have stated, the Anglo-American population may be unduly optimistic about their own life situation, an optimism that may be a cultural artifact. This optimism could affect both perceived vulnerability to earthquake hazards and the extent to which individuals prepare for future disaster. In addition, the extent to which hazard preparation is seen as an individual as opposed to a societal responsibility may also be a product of cultural context and may have important implications for changes in hazards mitigation policy. Future research must explicitly take into account the impacts of cultural values and assumptions on both perceived vulnerability and preparedness. Research in areas confronting similar geophysical risk, but occupied by different cultural groups, could be particularly fruitful in elucidating a better understanding of general as opposed to culturally specific responses.

A Final Word

California residents are aware of the earthquake risk that threatens lives and property. Many state and federal programs and much regulatory legislation have been adopted to prepare for a major earthquake and to reduce the loss of both life and property. However, large numbers of individuals have taken inadequate steps to protect themselves--to prepare their homes to withstand shaking, or to purchase and store supplies for the emergency hours following the earthquake. Our research suggests that a large percentage of the population is resistant to information and warnings. These findings forebode a large-scale disaster resulting partly from the lack of individual and household preparedness, a disaster that will accompany "the Great California Earthquake."

Appendix

Survey Questionnaire

Instructions: This set of questions will ask about your decision to purchase earthquake insurance as well as some other information about your household. Someone in your household may have responded to some of these questions in past surveys in 1989 and 1990. If possible, we would prefer that the same individual fill out this questionnaire.

It should take you no more than 15 minutes to complete this form.

We thank you for your cooperation - your responses are very important.

Q-1 Please circle all that apply:

YES	NO	Do you own the home listed at the address on the cover letter?
YES	NO	Is this your primary residence?
YES	NO	Have you lived at this address for at least the past 18 months?

IF YOU ANSWERED "NO" TO ANY OF THE ABOVE, PLEASE RETURN THIS FORM IN THE ENCLOSED STAMPED ENVELOPE. BY RETURNING THE QUESTIONNAIRE, WE WILL KNOW THAT WE SHOULD NOT CONTACT YOU AGAIN FOR THIS SURVEY. THANK YOU FOR YOUR HELP.

IF YOU ANSWERED "YES" TO ALL OF THE ABOVE, PLEASE CONTINUE ON TO QUESTION Q-2 ON PAGE 2.

Q-2. To your knowledge, has your present house or its contents ever suffered damage from an earthquake?

1. YES, IT HAS
   How much damage? $___________(dollar damage)
   In what year was that earthquake? _______________
2. NO, IT HASN'T
3. I DON'T KNOW

Q-3 Do you personally know anyone whose house or its contents has suffered damage from an earthquake within the last two years (excluding the 1989 San Francisco Bay area earthquake)?
1. YES
2. NO

Q-4. Have you personally experienced a frightening earthquake sometime within the past two years?
1. YES
2. NO

Q-5. In January of 1992, the State of California implemented a small surcharge to homeowner insurance bills to provide up to $15,000 (minus a small deductible) from a recovery fund for repairs to the home in the event of an earthquake.

Did you pay the surcharge for this coverage in 1992? (circle all of the numbers that apply)
1. YES **If yes,** why did you pay the premium? (circle one or more)

1. BECAUSE I THOUGHT IT WAS MANDATORY
2. BECAUSE I WANTED THIS EXTRA COVERAGE
3. I WORRIED THAT MY HOMEOWNERS POLICY WOULD BE CANCELED IF I DID NOT PAY THE SURCHARGE
4. OTHER

2. NO **If no,** why did you decide not to participate in this program? (circle the number of your answer)

1. THIS EXTRA PROTECTION IS NOT NECESSARY
2. THE ADDITIONAL FEE WAS TOO HIGH
3. BECAUSE OF STORIES IN THE NEWS MEDIA
4. BECAUSE OF MY INSURANCE BROKER
5. BECAUSE OF INFORMATION FROM FRIENDS,COLLEAGUES OR RELATIVES
6. I DON'T BELIEVE MY HOUSE WILL BE DAMAGED BY AN EARTHQUAKE
7. I DON'T THINK MY CLAIM WOULD BE HONORED IF I SUFFERED A LOSS
8. I HEARD THAT THE PROGRAM MAY BE CANCELED

9. OTHER (Please specify)____________________

Q-6. As you know, homeowners earthquake insurance is available as a separate policy from your insurance company. **Have you ever had** such a policy on this home? (circle the number of your answer)

1. YES 2. NO

Q-7. **Do you currently have** homeowner's earthquake insurance coverage on this home? (circle the number of your answer)

1. YES **[If yes, go to question Q-9.]**
2. NO

Answer this only if you do not have homeowners earthquake insurance.

Q-8. Why did you decide not to have earthquake insurance coverage? On a scale from 1 to 5 (1 is "not at all important" and 5 is "very important"), how important was each of the following in affecting your decision? (circle the number of your answer)

a I don't think that an earthquake will destroy my house or cause major damage in the near future.

not at all important **very important**
1 2 3 4 5

b. The cost of insurance was too high for me.
not at all important **very important**
1 2 3 4 5

c. Not much of our family wealth is tied up in the equity of our house, and so we have little to lose if an earthquake destroyed or damaged it.
not at all important **very important**
1 2 3 4 5

d. If a major earthquake occurs, the damage to my house will be less than the deductible on the insurance, so insurance is not a good buy.
not at all important **very important**
1 2 3 4 5

e. If a major earthquake occurs, the federal or state government will offer grants or loans that will be sufficient to rebuild my house, making insurance unnecessary.
not at all important **very important**
1 2 3 4 5

f. I am not confident that the insurance industry will actually pay out benefits if there is a major disaster.
not at all important **very important**
1 2 3 4 5

g. I know personally or have read about people who have not been able to collect fully from their insurance policies after disasters--and this has discouraged me from purchasing earthquake insurance.

not at all important **very important**
1 2 3 4 5

h. Because I paid the surcharge for the extra coverage the State of California is providing for the first $15,000 in damage.

not at all important **very important**
1 2 3 4 5

i. I watched a television program or read an article on earthquake hazards that convinced me that I didn't need to buy earthquake insurance.

not at all important **very important**
1 2 3 4 5

j. I saw newspaper maps showing hazards areas, and decided that I didn't need earthquake insurance.

not at all important **very important**
1 2 3 4 5

k. My neighbors (or the former owner, or friends, or relatives, or colleagues) convinced me not to buy it.

not at all important **very important**

l. My real estate agent suggested that I have it.

not at all important **very important**
1 2 3 4 5

m. My mortgage company or bank suggested that I have it.

not at all important **very important**
1 2 3 4 5

n. I felt the California Residential Earthquake Recovery Fund is sufficient and we didn't need homeowners' earthquake insurance coverage.

not at all important **very important**
1 2 3 4 5

o. Other (what?)____

not at all important **very important**
1 2 3 4 5

[Go to question Q-12 and continue]

Answer the following questions only if you <u>do</u> have private earthquake insurance.

Q-9. In what year did you get earthquake insurance on your present home?

______________________________(year)

Q-10. How much earthquake insurance coverage do you now have?
$ ____________________(write in the dollar amount)

Q-11. People take many things into account when they decide to buy earthquake insurance. On a scale from 1 to 5 (1 is "not at all important" and 5 is "very important"), how important was each of the following in affecting your decision to buy insurance? Circle the number.

a. I worry that an earthquake will destroy my house or cause major damage in the future.

not at all important **very important**

1 2 3 4 5

b. Most of our family wealth is tied up in the equity of our house, which might be lost if an earthquake destroyed or damaged it.

not at all important **very important**

1 2 3 4 5

c. The insurance salesperson convinced me that it is important to have earthquake insurance.

not at all important **very important**

1 2 3 4 5

d. My neighbors (or friends, relatives, colleagues) convinced me to have earthquake insurance.

not at all important **very important**

1 2 3 4 5

e. A letter or notice from the insurance company let me know that it was available--I decided to buy it.

not at all important **very important**

1 2 3 4 5

f. My real estate agent encouraged me to buy it.

not at all important **very important**

1 2 3 4 5

g. My mortgage lender suggested that I have it.

not at all important **very important**

1 2 3 4 5

h. I saw newspaper maps showing hazards areas, and decided I needed earthquake insurance.

not at all important **very important**

1 2 3 4 5

i. The fact that the State of California enacted a program to cover the first $15,000 of earthquake damage called my attention to the need for full insurance coverage.

not at all important **very important**

1 2 3 4 5

j. I watched a television program or read an article on earthquake hazards that convinced me to buy earthquake insurance.

not at all important **very important**

1 2 3 4 5

k. If a major earthquake occurs, the damage to my house will be very great, so insurance is a good buy.

not at all important **very important**
1 2 3 4 5

l. If a major earthquake occurs, the grants or loans available from the federal or state government will not be sufficient to rebuild my house.

not at all important **very important**
1 2 3 4 5

m. I am confident that the insurance industry will pay out benefits if there is a major disaster.

not at all important **very important**
1 2 3 4 5

n. I know personally or have read about people who were able to collect fully from their insurance policies after disasters - and this has encouraged me to purchase earthquake insurance.

not at all important **very important**
1 2 3 4 5

o. The repeal of the California Residential Earthquake Recovery Fund called my attention to the fact that we needed homeowners earthquake insurance coverage.

not at all important **very important**
1 2 3 4 5

p. Other (what?)______________________________

not at all important **very important**
1 2 3 4 5

Please answer all of the following regardless of whether or not you have earthquake insurance.

Q-12. In your opinion, which county (or counties) in California are most susceptible to major damage from earthquakes?

____
(county names)

Q-13. Have you done anything to reduce the amount of damage and disruption an earthquake might cause?

1. YES If **"YES,"** what did you do? (check answers)

Structural Measures

_____ Braced, strapped and anchored the water heater
_____ Anchored or bolted the house to the foundation
_____ Braced and reinforced cripple walls
_____ Strengthened the house's exterior foundation or unreinforced masonry exterior walls
_____ Strengthened the garage door opening

Other Measures to Prepare for an earthquake
___ Stored food and water
___ Maintain emergency supplies including flashlight, portable battery-operated radio, medicines,first-aid kit
___ Secured heavy appliances, furniture, mirrors, etc.
___ Know how to shut off gas, water, electricity
___ Made plans for family reunion after earthquake
___ Conducted practice drills
___ Have tools such as pipe wrench for turning off gas, water and fire extinguisher
___ Other (Please specify) ______________________________

Q-14. Some people have estimated the chances of a strong earthquake (of the size that struck San Francisco in 1906) happening in southern California in the next 10 years as 1 out of 5.
Now, please think about the chances of a San Francisco-type earthquake occurring in your community. What do you think are the chances that such an earthquake would occur in the next ten years in your community?

1 out of ______________________ (number)

Q-15. How likely do you think it is that your own home will be seriously damaged by an earthquake in the next ten years? (circle number).

1. VERY LIKELY
2. SOMEWHAT LIKELY
3. SOMEWHAT UNLIKELY
4. NOT VERY LIKELY

Q-16. What are the chances of a 1906 San Francisco-type earthquake causing more than 10 percent damage to your own home in the next 10 years. One out of how many is your estimate of the chances of such an earthquake occurring in the next ten years?

1 out of ______________________(number)

Q-17. Suppose a major damaging earthquake occurred in your community - of the magnitude of the 1906 San Francisco earthquake. How much (in dollars) damage would be caused to the contents of your house as well as the house itself?

$____

(dollar value of damage to the house and contents)

Finally, we would like to ask a few questions about your household for statistical purposes.

Q-21. How long have you lived in California?
_________________ **(years)**

Q-22. How long has your household lived at this address?
______________________(years)

Q-23 Which description best matches your current home
1. Single-family detached dwelling
2. Townhouse or condominium
3. Planned unit development (PUD)
4. Other (what)____________________

Q-24. Are you male_____ female_____ ?

Q-25 What is your age? ___________ (years)

Q-26. How many years of school have you completed?
_____________ (years of school completed)

Q-27. How many persons, total, live in this household?
_______________(# of persons in household)

Q-28. How many children under the age of 18 live in your house?
_______________(# of children)

Q-29. How many persons over the age of 65 live in your house?
_______________(# over 65)

Q-30 How much do you think your home (house and lot) would sell for if it were for sale?

$_____________________(current market value of your house)

Q-31. How much do you now owe on your house?

$_____________________(total outstanding mortgages)

Q-32. Approximately what was your total gross family income from all sources before taxes in 1992? (circle the number)

1. OVER $150,000
2. $100,000-$149,999
3. $50,000- $99,999
4. $30,000-$49,999
5. $20,000-$29,000
6. $15,000-$19,999
7. UNDER $15,000

Q-33. Did the California Residential Earthquake Recover Fund have an impact on your decision to purchase earthquake insurance?

1. YES 2. NO

Q-34. Should the State of California reconsider and enact a mandatory earthquake program to provide damage coverage for homeowners at a premium cost of between $15 and $75 per year?

1. YES

If Yes, should homeowners also be required to take loss reduction measures such as fixing foundations and anchoring water heaters in order to get this coverage?

1. YES 2. NO 3. DON'T KNOW

2. NO
3. DON'T KNOW

Q-35. Did you personally respond to a similar survey from us in 1989?

1. YES 2. NO 3. DON'T REMEMBER

Q-36. Did you personally respond to a similar survey from us again in 1990?

1. YES 2. NO 3. DON'T REMEMBER

Please return your completed questionnaire in the enclosed stamped envelope. THANK YOU FOR YOUR PARTICIPATION IN THIS SURVEY.

References

Ajzen, I., and M. Fishbein. 1977. "Attitude-behavior relations: A theoretical analysis of review of empirical research." *Psychological Bulletin*, 84:888-918.

Alesch, D.J., and William J. Petak. 1986. *The Politics and Economics of Earthquake Hazard Mitigation*. Boulder: University of Colorado, Institute of Behavioral Science, Monograph # 43.

Alexander, David. 1993. *Natural Disasters*. New York: Chapman and Hall.

Anderson, Dan, and Maurice Weinrobe. 1981. *Geographic Mortgage Risk: Implications for the Federal Home Loan Mortgage Corporation*. Washington, D.C.: Kaplan, Smith & Associates.

Andrisani, Paul J. 1980. "Introduction and overview." *Journal of Economics and Business*. Special issue on Longitudinal Research and Labor Force Behavior, 32(2):89-93.

Arrow, Kenneth J. 1970. "The Theory of Risk Aversion." In Kenneth Arrow, ed., *Essays in the Theory of Risk-Bearing*. Pp. 90-109. New York: North-Holland.

Asch, S. E. 1956. "Studies of independence and conformity: A minority of one against a unanimous majority." *Psychological Monograph*, 70.

Ashenfelter, Orley, and Gary Solon. 1982. "Longitudinal Labor Markets and Limitations." In *What's Happening to Labor Force and Productivity Measurements? Proceedings of a June 17, 1982, Conference Sponsored by the National Council on Employment Policy*. Pp. 109-126. Kalamazoo, MI: W.E. Upjohn Institute for Employment Research.

Averill, J. R. 1987. "The Role of Emotions and Psychological Defense in Self-Protective Behavior." In N. D. Weinstein, ed., *Taking Care: Understanding and Encouraging Self-Protective Behavior*. Pp. 54-78. New York: Cambridge University Press.

Baker, Earl, J. 1979. "Predicting Response to Hurricane Warnings: A reanalysis of data from four studies." *Mass Emergencies*, 4:9-24.

Berman, J. J. 1990. *Cross-cultural perspectives: Nebraska Symposium on Motivation*. Lincoln, NE: University of Nebraska Press.

Bjorklund, Anders. 1989. "Potentials and pitfalls of panel data: the case of job mobility." *European Economic Review,* 33:537-546.

Blanchard, R. Denise. 1992. "Impact of the 1990 Revised Earthquake Prediction for the San Francisco Bay Area: Risk Communication and Individual Response Behavior." Unpublished Ph.D. dissertation, University of Colorado, Department of Geography.

Bogard, William C. 1988. "Bringing social theory to hazards research: conditions and consequences of the mitigation of environmental hazards." *Sociological Perspectives,* 31:147-168.

Bolt, Bruce. 1993. *Earthquakes.* New York: W. H. Freeman.

Brabb, Earl A., and J. A. Olsen. 1986. *Map showing faults and earthquake epicenters in San Mateo County, California.* U.S. Geological Survey Miscellaneous Investigations Series Map I-1257-F.

Brown, James. 1987. Using the insurance and finance industries to influence purchase of earthquake insurance: antitrust considerations. Unpublished paper presented to a workshop sponsored by the George Washington University under contract with the Federal Emergency Management Agency, Boulder, Colorado, July 17-18, 1987.

Bryant, E. A. 1991. *Natural Hazards.* Cambridge: Cambridge University Press.

Burton, Ian and Robert W. Kates. 1964. "The perception of natural hazards in Resource Management." *Natural Resources Journal,* 3:412-441.

California Seismic Safety Commission. 1992. *The Homeowner's Guide to Earthquake Safety.* Sacramento: California Seismic Safety Commission.

Cialdini, R. B. 1988. *Influence: Science and Practice.* Glenview, IL: Scott, Foresman.

Committee on Earthquake and Environmental Sciences. 1992. *Reducing the Impacts of Natural Hazards: A Strategy for the Nation.* Washington, D.C.: Committee on Earth and Environmental Sciences, Subcommittee on Natural Disaster Reduction, Office of Science and Technology Policy.

Cordray, Sheila Mary. 1982. The problem of attrition in longitudinal survey research. Unpublished Ph.D. dissertation, Department of Sociology, University of Oregon.

Cross, John A. 1990. "Longitudinal changes in hurricane hazard perception." *International Journal of Mass Emergencies and Disasters.* 8:31-47.

Cutter, Susan. 1993. *Living with Risk: Geography of Technological Hazards.* London: Edward Arnold.

Cutter, Susan L., John Tiefenbacher, and William D. Solecki. 1994. "En-gendered fears: Femininity and technological risk perception" in Susan Cutter, ed., *Environmental Risks and Hazards.* Pp. 137-149. Englewood Cliffs, N.J.: Prentice-Hall.

Davies, R. B. 1987. "The limitations of cross sectional analysis" in Robert Crouchley, ed., *Longitudinal Data Analysis.* Pp. 1-15. Aldershot: Avebury.

Dillman, Don. 1978. *Mail and Telephone Surveys: The Total Design Method.* New York: Wiley.

Dornic, Stanislav. 1967. *Subjective Distance and Emotional Involvement: A Verification of the Exponent Invariance.* Reports from the Psychological Laboratories, No. 237. Stockholm: University of Stockholm.

Drabek, Thomas. 1986. *Human System Responses to Disaster: An Inventory of Sociological Findings.* New York: Springer-Verlag.

Earthquake Engineering Research Institute. 1992. Cape Mendocino, California, April 25-26. 1992. *EERI Newsletter,* Special Earthquake Report, 26 (6):5.

_______. 1992. Landers and Big Bear Earthquakes of June 18 and 29. 1992. *EERI Newsletter,* Special Earthquake Report, 26 (8):1.

Edwards, W. 1955. "The Prediction of Decisions among Bets." *Journal of Experimental Psychology,* 50:201-214.

Einhorn, Hillel and Robin Hogarth. 1985. "Ambiguity and Uncertainty in Probabilistic Inference." *Psychological Review,* 92:433-461.

Fazio, R. H. and M. P. Zanna. 1978. "Attitudinal qualities relating to the strength of the attitude-behavior relationship." *Journal of Experimental Social Psychology,* 14:398-408.

Federal Emergency Management Agency. 1980. *An assessment of the consequences and preparations for a catastrophic California earthquake: findings and actions taken.* Washington, D.C.: Federal Emergency Management Agency.

Friedman, M., and L. J. Savage. 1948. "The Utility Analysis of Choices Involving Risk." *Journal of Political Economy,* 56:279-304.

Geipel, Robert. 1982. *Disaster and Reconstruction: The Friuli (Italy) Earthquakes of 1976.* London: Allen & Unwin.

Gere, James M., and Haresh C. Shah. 1984. *Terra Non Firma: Understanding and Preparing for Earthquakes.* Stanford, CA: Stanford Alumni Association.

Goldstein, W. M., and Hillel J. Einhorn. 1987. "Expression Theory and the Preference Reversal Phenomena." *Psychological Review,* 94:236-254.

Gould, Peter. 1966. On Mental Maps. *Michigan Inter-University Community of Mathematical Geographers*: 9.

Gould, Peter, and Rodney White. 1986. *Mental Maps,* 2nd ed. Winchester, MA: Allen & Unwin.

Greene, Marjorie, Ronald Perry, and Michael Lindell. 1981. "The March 1980 Eruptions of Mt. St. Helens: Citizen Perceptions of Volcano Threat." *Disasters,* 5(1):49-66.

Hagenaars, Jacques A. 1990. *Categorical Longitudinal Data: Log-linear panel, trend and cohort analysis.* Newbury Park, CA: Sage Publications.

Hanson, Susan, John D. Vitek, and Perry O. Hanson. 1979. "Awareness of Tornadoes: the importance of an historic event." *Journal of Geography,* 78:22-25.

Harvey, David. 1989. *The Condition of Post-Modernity.* Oxford: Basil Blackwell.

Harway, M., S., A. Mednick, and B. Mednick. 1984. "Research Strategies: Methodological and Practical Problems" in Eds. Sarnoff A. Mednick, Michele Harway, and Karen M. Finello, *Handbook of Longitudinal Research, Vol. One, Birth and Childhood Cohorts*. Pp. 22-30. New York: Praeger.

Harwood, Bruce, and Charles J. Jacobus. 1990. *Real Estate Principles*, 5th ed. Englewood Cliffs, NJ: Prentice-Hall.

Hodge, David, Virginia Sharp, and Marion Marts. 1979. "Contemporary Responses to Volcanism: Case Studies from the Cascades and Hawaii." In Payson D. Sheets and Donald K. Grayson, eds., *Volcanic Activity and Human Ecology*. Pp. 221-248. New York: Academic Press.

Hogarth, Robin M., and Howard Kunreuther. 1993. "Decision making under ignorance: arguing with yourself." University of Pennsylvania, Risk Management and Decision Processes Center, Paper #93-10-04.

Holden, Richard, and Charles R. Real. 1990. *Seismic Hazard Information Needs of the Insurance Industry, Local Government and Property Owners in California: An Analysis.* Sacramento, CA: California Department of Conservation, Division of Mines and Geology, Special Publication #108.

Holzer, Thomas L. 1994. "Loma Prieta Damage Largely Attributed to Enhanced Ground Shaking." *EOS, Transactions, American Geophysical Union* 75(26):299-301.

Hujer, Reinhard, and Hilmer Schneider. 1989. "The analysis of labor market mobility using panel data." *European Economic Review* 33:530-536.

Iacopi, Robert. 1978. *Earthquake Country: How, Why, and Where Earthquakes Strike in California.* Menlo Park, CA: Lane Books.

Janis, I. L.. 1967. "Effect of Fear Arousal on Attitude Change: Recent Developments in Theory and Experimental Research." In L. Berkowitz, ed., *Advances in Experimental Social Psyghology.* Pp. 166-224. New York: Academic Press.

Janoff-Budman, R. 1985. "Criminal vs. Noncriminal Victimization: Victims' Reactions." *Victimology* 10:498-511.

Johnson, Brandon B., and Vincent T. Covello, eds. 1987. *The Social and Cultural Construction of Risk.* Dordrecht: Reidel.

Johnson, Eric J., J. W. Payne, and J. R. Bettman. 1988. "Information Displays and Preference Reversals, "*Organizational Behavior and Human Decision Processes* 42:1-21.

Joint Committee on Seismic Safety. 1974. *Meeting the Earthquake Challenge: Final Report to the Legislature of the State of California.* Sacramento, CA: Joint Committee on Seismic Safety.

Kahneman, D., and Amos Tversky. 1979. "Prospect Theory: an analysis of decision under risk." *Econometrica.* 47(2):263-291.

Kasperson, Roger, E., Ortwin Renn, Paul Slovic, Halina S. Brown, Jacque Emel, Robert Goble, Jeanne X. Kasperson, and Samuel Ratick. 1988. "The Social Amplification of Risk: A conceptual framework." *Risk Analysis* 8:177-187.

Kates, Robert W. 1971. "Natural Hazard in Human Ecological Perspective: Hypotheses and Models." *Economic Geography* 47:438-451.

Kessler, Ronald C., and David F. Greenberg. 1981. *Linear Panel Analysis: Models of Quantitative Change.* New York: Academic Press.

Klevmarken, N. Anders. 1989. "Panel Studies: What Can We Learn from Them?" *European Economic Review* 33: 523-529.

Kunreuther, Howard, Neil Ericksen, and John Handmer. 1993. "Reducing Losses from Natural Disasters through insurance and mitigation: a cross-cultural comparison." University of Pennsylvania, Risk Management and Decision Processes Center, Publication 93-10-01.

Kunreuther, Howard, R. Ginsberg, L. Miller, P. Sagi, P. Slovic, B. Borkan, and N. Katz. 1978. *Disaster Insurance Protection: Public Policy Lessons.* New York: Wiley.

Lazarsfeld, Paul F., B. Berelson, and H. Gaudet. 1948. *The People's Choice.* New York: Columbia University Press.

Leik, Robert K., Sheila A. Leik, Knut Ekker, and Gergory A. Gifford. 1982. "Under the Threat of Mount St. Helens, A Study of Chronic Family Stress." Minneapolis: Family Study Center, University of Minnesota.

Ley, David. 1983. *A Social Geography of the City.* New York: Harper and Row.

Lichtenstein, Sarah and Paul Slovic. 1971. "Reversals of Preference between Bids and Choices in Gambling Decisions." *Journal of Experimental Psychology* 89: 46-55.

Lindh, A. G. 1983. *A preliminary assessment of long-term probabilities for large earthquakes along selected fault segments of the San Andreas fault system.* U.S. Geological Survey Open-File Report 83-63:15.

Lukermann, Fred. 1961. "The role of theory in geographical inquiry." *Professional Geographer* 13:1-6.

Marden, Peter. 1992. "The deconstructionist tendencies of postmodern geographies." *Progress in Human Geography* 16: 41-57.

Markus, H., and Kitayama, S. 1991. "Culture and the self: Implications for cognition, emotion, and motivation." *Psychological Review* 98:224-253.

_______. 1992. The what, why and how of cultural psychology: A review of R. Shweder's *Thinking through Cultures. Psychological Inquiry,* 3, 357-364.

Mattingly, Shirley. 1987. "Response and Recovery Planning with Consideration of the Scenario Earthquakes Developed by California Division of Mines and Geology." In *Proceedings of Conference 41: A Review of Earthquake Research Applications in the National Earthquake Hazards Reduction Program: 1977-1987.* Pp. 550-554. Reston, VA: U.S. Geological Survey, Open File Report 88-13-A.

McNutt, Stephen R., and Robert H. Sydnor, eds. 1990. *The Loma Prieta (Santa Cruz Mountains), California Earthquake of 17 October 1989.* Sacramento, CA: Department of Conservation, Division of Mines and Geology, Special Publication #104.

Mednick, S. A., and B. Mednick. 1984. "A Brief History of North American Longitudinal Research." In Sarnoff A. Mednick, Michele Harway, and Karen M. Finello, eds., *Handbook of Longitudinal Research, Vol. 1, Birth and Childhood Cohorts* . Pp. 18-22. New York: Praeger .

Meltsner, Arnold J. 1978. "Public support for seismic safety: where is it in California." *Mass Emergencies* 3:167-184.

Mileti, Dennis S., and Colleen Fitzpatrick. 1993. *The Great Earthquake Experiment: Risk Communication and Public Action.* Boulder, CO: Westview Press.

Morgan, James N., Katherine Dickinson, Jonathan Dickinson, Jacob Benus, and Greg Duncan, eds. 1974. "Introduction." *Five Thousand American Families - - Patterns of Economic Progress,* Vol. 1, An Analysis of the First Five Years of the Panel Study of Income Dynamics. Pp. 1-9. Ann Arbor, MI: Survey Research Center of the Institute for Social Research, University of Michigan.

Mosteller, F., and P. Nogee. 1941. "An Experimental Measurement of Utility." *Journal of Political Economy*, 59: 371-404.

Mumford, Michael, Garnett S. Stokes, and William A. Owens. 1990. *Patterns of Life History: The ecology of human individuality.* Hillsdale, NJ: Lawrence Erlbaum Associates.

Myers, D. 1993. *Social psychology,* 4th ed. New York: McGraw-Hill.

National Academy of Engineering. 1969. *Earthquake Engineering Research.* Washington, D.C.: National Academy of Sciences.

National Research Council. 1969. *Toward Reduction of Losses from Earthquakes: Conclusions from the Great Alaska Earthquake of 1964.* Washington, D.C.: National Academy of Sciences.

Needham, Joseph. 1959. *Science and Civilisation in China.* Vol. 3, Mathematics and the Sciences of the Heavens and the Earth. Cambridge: Cambridge University Press.

Nisbett, R. E., and L. Ross. 1980. *Human Inference: Strategies and Shortcomings.* Englewood Cliffs, NJ: Prentice-Hall.

Norusis, Marija J. 1990. *SPSSx Advanced Statistics Guide.* New York: McGraw-Hill.

Olson, Robert A., Constance Holland, H. Grana Millers, W. Henry Lambright, Henry J. Lagorio, and Carl R. Treseder. 1988. *To Save Lives and Protect Property: A Policy Assessment of Federal Earthquake Activities, 1964-1987.* Sacramento, CA: VSP Associates.

Orme, Anthony. 1992. "The San Andreas Fault" In Don Janelle, ed., *Geographical Snapshots of North America.* Pp. 145-149. New York and London: Guilford.

Palm, Risa, and Michael E. Hodgson. 1993. Natural Hazards in Puerto Rico: Attitudes, Experience, and Behavior of Homeowners. Boulder, CO: University of Colorado, Institute of Behavioral Science Monograph #55.

_______. 1992. *After a California Earthquake: Attitude and Behavior Change.* Chicago: University of Chicago Press.

Palm, Risa. 1981. *Real Estate Agents and Special Studies Zones Disclosure: The Response of California Home Buyers to Earthquake Hazards Information.* Monograph #32. Boulder, CO: University of Colorado, Program on Technology, Environment and Man.

Palm, Risa, Michael Hodgson, Denise Blanchard and Donald Lyons. 1990. *Earthquake Insurance in California: Environmental Policy and Individual Decision-Making.* Boulder, CO: Westview Press.

Perkins, J. B. 1987. *Maps showing cumulative damage potential from earthquake ground shaking, San Mateo County, California.* U.S. Geological Survey Miscellaneous Investigations Series Map I-1267-I.

Perloff, L. S. 1983. "Perceptions of Vulnerability to Victimization." *Journal of Social Issues* 39:41-61.

Petty, R. E., and Cacioppo, J. T. 1986. *Communication and persuasion: Central and peripheral routes to attitude change.* New York: Springer-Verlag.

Porteous, J. D. 1976. "Home: The Territorial core." *Geographical Review* 66: 383-390.

Roder, Wolf. 1961. "Attitudes and Knowledge on the Topeka Flood Plain." In G. F. White, ed., *Papers on Flood Problems,* Chicago: University of Chicago, Department of Geography, Research Paper #70.

Roth, Richard. 1990. "The New California Residential Earthquake Recovery Fund and the Need for a Federal Earthquake Recovery Program." In *Hearings before the Subcommittee on Policy Research and Insurance of the Committee on Banking, Finance and Urban Affairs, House of Representatives, Serial # 101-168*, Pp. 830-836. Washington, D.C.: Government Printing Office.

Saarinen, Thomas F. 1982. *Environmental Planning: Perception and Behavior.* Boston: Houghton Mifflin.

Schaie, K. Warner. 1983. "What can we learn from the longitudinal study of adult psychological development?" in K. Warner Schaie, ed., *Longitudinal Studies of Adult Psychological Development.* Pp. 1-19. New York and London: Guilford .

Schiff, Myra. 1977. "Hazard Adjustment, Locus of Control, and Sensation Seeking: Some Null Findings." *Environment and Behavior* 9(6):233-254.

Schkade, David A., and Eric J. Johnson. 1989. "Cognitive Processes in Preference Reversals." *Organizational Behavior and Human Decision Processes,* 44: 203-231.

Shimada, Kazuo. 1972. "Attitudes toward Disaster Defense Organizations and Volunteer Activities in Emergencies. In *Proceedings of the Japan-United States Disaster Research Seminar: Organizational and Community Responses to Disasters.* Pp. 208-217. Columbus, OH: The Ohio State University, Disaster Research Center.

Shoji, Saito. 1983. "Catfishes" in *Kodansha Encyclopedia of Japan,* 1st ed. Tokyo and New York: Kodansha, vol. 5., 249.

Shweder, R. A.,1991. *Cultural Psychology: Thinking through cultures.* Cambridge, MA: Harvard University Press.

Shweder, R. A., and LeVine, R. A. 1984. *Culture theory: Essays on mind, self, and emotion.* New York: Cambridge University Press.

Simpson-Housley, Paul, and Peter Bradshaw. 1978. "Personality and the Perception of Earthquake Hazard." *Australian Geographical Studies,* 16:65-72.

Slovic, Paul. 1986. "Informing and Educating the Public About Risk." *Risk Analysis* 6:403-415.

_______. 1987. "Perception of Risk." *Science,* 236:280-285.

Slovic, Paul, Baruch Fischoff, Sarah Lichtenstein, B. Corrigan, and B. Combs. 1977. "Preference for insuring against probable small losses: insurance implications." *Journal of Risk and Insurance,* 44: 237-258.

Slovic, Paul, Howard Kunreuther, and Gilbert F. White. 1974. "Decision Processes, Rationality and Adjustment to Natural Hazards." In G. F. White, ed., *Natural Hazards: Local, National and Global.* Pp. 187-205. New York: Oxford University Press.

Smith, Keith. 1992. *Environmental Hazards: Assessing Risk and Reducing Disaster.* London and New York: Routledge.

Sontag, Lester W. 1971. "The history of longitudinal research: implications for the future." *Child Development* 42: 987-1002.

Sopher, David E. 1978. "The Structuring of Space in Place Names and Words for Place." In David Ley and Marwyn S. Samuels, eds., *Humanistic Geography: Prospects and Problems.* Pp. 251-268. London: Croom Helm.

_______. 1979. "The Landscape of Home." In Donald Meinig, ed., *The Interpretation of Ordinary Landscapes.* Pp. 129-149. New York: Oxford University Press.

Steinbrugge, Karl, et al. 1981. *Metropolitan San Francisco and Los Angeles Earthquake Loss Studies: 1980 Assessment.* Reston, VA: U.S. Geological Survey, Open File Report 81-113.

Stigler, J. W., Shweder, R. A., and Herdt, G., eds. 1991. *Cultural psychology: Essays on comparative human development.* London: Cambridge University Press.

Suttmeier, Richard P. 1994. "Risk in China: Comparative and Historical perspectives on its social construction and management." *Technological Forecasting and Social Change.* 45.

Thiel, Charles C., Jr., ed. 1990. *Competing Against Time.* Northern Highlands, CA: California Office of Planning and Research.

Thier, Herbert D. 1988. "The California Earthquake Education Program." In Walter W. Hays, ed., *Proceedings of Conference 41: A Review of Earthquake Research Applications in the National Earthquake Hazards Reduction Program: 1977-1987.* Pp. 65-74. Reston, VA: U.S. Geological Survey, Open File Report 88-13-A.

Thomson, J. M., and J. F. Evernden. 1986. *Map showing predicted seismic-shaking intensities of an earthquake in San Mateo County, California, comparable in magnitude to the 1906 San Francisco earthquake.* U.S. Geological Survey Miscellaneous Investigations Series Map I-1257-H.

Tobin, L. Thomas. 1988. "Senate Bill 547: California Legislation as a Research Application." In Walter W. Hays, ed., *Proceedings of Conference 41: A Review of Earthquake Research Applications in the National Earthquake Hazards Reduction Program: 1977-1987.* Pp. 241-258. Reston, VA: U.S. Geological Survey, Open File Report 88-13-A.

Tuan, Yi-Fu. 1974. *Topophilia: A Study of Environmental Perception, Attitudes, and Values.* Englewood Cliffs, NJ: Prentice-Hall.

Turner, Ralph, Joanne Nigg, Denise Paz, and Barbara Young. 1981. "Community Response to Earthquake Threat in Southern California. Part 10, Summary and Recommendations. Los Angeles: Institute for Social Science Research, University of California, Los Angeles.

_______. 1979. *Earthquake Threat: The Human Response in Southern California.* Los Angeles: Institute for Social Science Research, University of California, Los Angeles.

Tversky, Amos, and D. Kahneman. 1974. "Judgement Under Uncertainty: Heuristics and Biases," *Science* 185: 1124-1131.

_______. 1981. "The Framing of Decisions and the Psychology of Choice." *Science,* 211:453-458.

Vance, James E., Jr. 1972. "California and the Search for the Ideal." *Annals, Association of American Geographers,* 62: 185-210.

Ward, Peter L. 1990, *The Next Big Earthquake in the Bay Area May Come Sooner Than You think.* Menlo Park, CA: U.S. Geological Survey.

Ward, Peter L., and Robert A. Page. 1990. *The Loma Prieta Earthquake of October 17, 1989: What Happened, What is Expected, What Can Be Done."* Washington, D.C.: U.S. Geological Survey.

Warwick, Donald, and Charles Lininger. 1975. *The Sample Survey: Theory and Practice.* New York: McGraw-Hill.

Weinstein, N. D. 1989a. "Effects of Personal Experience on Self-Protective Behavior." *Psychological Bulletin* 105:31-50.

_______. 1989b. "Optimistic Biases About Personal Risks." *Science* 246:1232-33.

_______. 1987. "Unrealistic optimism about illness susceptibility: Conclusions from a community-wide sample." *Journal of Behavioral Medicine* 10:481-500.

Wesson, R. L., and R. E. Wallace. 1985. "Predicting the next great earthquake in California." *Scientific American*, 252(2): 35-43.

White, Gilbert F., ed. 1974. *Natural Hazards: Local, National, Global.* New York: Oxford University Press.

White, Gilbert F., 1994. "A Perspective on Reducing Losses from Natural Hazards." *Bulletin of the American Meterological Society 75(7): 1237-1240.*

Wieczorek, G. F., R. C. Wilson, and E. L. Harp. 1985. *Map showing slope stability during earthquakes in San Mateo County, California.* U.S. Geological Survey Miscellaneous Investigations Series Map I-1257-E.

Wildavsky, Aaron, and Karl Dake. 1990. "Theories of risk perception: who fears what and why?" Daedalus 119(4):41-60, Reprinted in Susan Cutter, ed. 1994, *Environmental Risks and Hazards*. Pp. 166-177. Englewood Cliffs, NJ Prentice-Hall.

Willinger, Marc. 1989. "Risk Aversion and the Value of Information." *Journal of Risk and Insurance* 56:320-328.

Windham, G. O., E. I. Posey, P. J. Ross, and B. G. Spencer. 1978. *Reactions to Storm Threat During Hurricane Eloise.* Social Science Research Center, Report 51. State College, Mississippi: Mississippi State University.

Working Group on the Probabilities of Future Large Earthquakes in Southern California. 1992. *Future Seismic Hazards in Southern California, Phase I: Implications of the 1992 Landers Earthquake Sequence.* Sacramento, CA: California Division of Mines and Geology.

Wylie, L. A., Jr., and J. R. Filson. 1989. "Armenia earthquake reconnaissance report." *Earthquake Spectra* 5.

Yerkes, R. F. 1985. "Geologic and seismologic setting." In J. I. Ziony, ed., *Evaluating Earthquake Hazards in the Los Angeles Region: An Earth-Science Perspective*. Pp. 25-42. Washington, D.C.: U.S. Geological Survey Professional Paper 1360.

Youd, T. L., and J. B. Perkins. 1987. *Map showing liquefaction susceptibility of San Mateo County, California.* U.S. Geological Survey Miscellaneous Investigations Series Map I-1257-G.

Ziony, J. I., and Kockelman, William J. 1985. "Introduction." In J. I. Ziony, ed., *Evaluating Earthquake Hazards in the Los Angeles Region: An Earth-Science Perspective.* Pp. 1-14. Washington, D.C.: U.S. Geological Survey Professional Paper 1360.

Ziony, J. I., and R. F. Yerkes. 1985. "Evaluating Earthquake and Surface-Faulting Potential" In J. I. Ziony, ed., *Evaluating Earthquake Hazards in the Los Angeles Region: An Earth-Science Perspective.* Pp. 43-92. Washington, D.C.: U.S. Geological Survey Professional Paper 1360.

Index